MW00790878

Cover to Cover

"The basic nuts and bolts of what every first-time writer needs to get their book ready. Simply a must-use resource—entertaining too. Sandy is a god."

—**Chris Meyer,** Amazon best-selling author of
The 'Wood, *Life in 20 Lessons,* and the upcoming
Four Months … and a Lifetime

"New authors: Relax, read, and be empowered. Sandra Wendel's knowledge of the editing process, peppered with humor, straightens your publishing path. Irreverent at times, succinct, the guide any serious first-time author needs."

—**Barbara Lynn Vannoy,** author of the award-winning
The 10 Greatest Gifts We Give Each Other:
A Memoir on the Magic of Marriage Vows

"Sandra Wendel, author, college teacher, and first-class editor. I know Sandra is first class because I watched her edit my books—book after book. I love not just her excellent professionalism but also her humor. Her *Cover to Cover* is often amusing—with just a bit of a bite. You'll find out what to do with your book that needs editing, and you'll also receive candid information about the publishing world you'll be entering. I think you'll learn a lot about getting the words right."

—**Marilyn June Coffey,** Great Plains writer, prolific author
of award-winning nonfiction and prize-winning
poetry on controversial topics

"As a new author, working with Sandra as an editor was like taking a breath of fresh air. She guided me through the editing and publishing process to create a beautiful, award-winning book. Her frank and honest advice about preparing your book for editing and publishing will keep you moving forward in the right direction. Sandra shares details, secrets, and years of knowledge that will help new (and experienced) authors be successful."

—**Sheryl Ness,** author of *Love in a Tuscan Kitchen: Savoring Life Through the Romance, Recipes, and Traditions of Italy*

"When I was at this stage with my book, this would have been exactly what I needed. I searched for other resources but could not find anything as comprehensive as what Sandra's book delivers."

—**Dennis Geelen,** author of *The Zero In Formula*

"I approached this endeavor without any working knowledge of the process to the extent that I didn't even know what my most pressing questions were. Really everything from types of edits (covered in this book), grammatical correctness (covered), other professionals to work with such as designers (covered), publishing (introduced), and marketing (introduced)."

—**Scott Rossignol,** aspiring first-time author, alternative elementary school principal

"This book is exactly what any author looking for an editor needs. If you want to produce a solid book, you need an editor. But how do you find an editor? What do you pay? What will they do for you? Sandy answers every question you have in this funny, straight to-the-point, quick, easy read packed with everything you need to find and build a solid relationship with your editor."

—**Jenny Kate**, marketing expert, author of *Social Media for Authors: Book Marketing for Authors Who'd Rather Write,* and founder of Writer Nation, www.thewriternation.com

"I felt like I was talking to Sandra again in our first meeting (as I read this book). And having that conversation gave me comfort in what I was doing. She was honest, patient, and informative, yet direct and transparent, too, shown through her style, stories, and factual approach to editing."

—**Catherine Rymsha, EdD,** author of *The Leadership Decision,* a lecturer on leadership at the University of Massachusetts, Lowell with a TEDx Talk: "Want to Become a Better Leader? Here's How. Just Listen"

"There are scores of books on writing and publishing, but Sandra Wendel cuts through the BS for first-time authors. *Cover to Cover* is a fantastic power tool for working with an editor, and it's also a lot of fun to read."

—**Lisa Pelto,** Founder & President, Concierge Publishing Services

"First-time authors need help, and this book explains, patiently, the many how-tos and don't-dos for aspiring authors to get their books from idea to reader. I applaud Sandra Wendel for creating a guide that so many of our authors need."

—**Michele DeFilippo,** Owner, 1106 Design

"Sandra is world-class at her craft. As a first-time author, I could not be more grateful that tate paired me with Sandra to get the editing done. Not only did she save me a lot of money, time, and frustration, she also went above and beyond with her wealth of knowledge to make sure the final product was the best it could possibly be. *Cover to Cover* is a game changer, especially for those who have no idea where to get started with the intricate book publishing process."

—**John Stankiewicz,** 7-figure Sales Team Leader, podcaster, and author of *Beyond the Classroom: The Unconventional Education of an Entrepreneur*

"Before I was an author, I was just a guy with a very rough manuscript that needed the services of an editor, badly. Sandra Wendel helped me through every step of getting published and into marketing. I would have been lost without her guidance. Her skills and knowledge of the industry are beyond impressive."

—**Richard Stanley,** bank robber, author of *Up on Game: When I Ruled the World* and *Up on Game: From Robbing Banks to Stacking Bitcoin* and called "one of the most fascinating people I have ever interviewed" by Adam Carolla (#1 podcast)

Cover to Cover

What *First-Time* Authors Need to Know about Editing

Read _this_ book before you publish _your_ book.

Insider Secrets Nobody Ever Tells You

Sandra Wendel
Editor, Write On, Inc.

Write On Ink Publishing
Omaha, Nebraska

Books by Sandra Wendel

*How Not to Be My Patient: A Physician's Secrets for
Staying Healthy and Surviving Any Diagnosis*
(Edward T. Creagan, MD, Mayo Clinic, with Sandra Wendel)

*Farewell: Vital End-of-Life Questions with Candid Answers
from a Leading Palliative and Hospice Physician*
(Edward T. Creagan, MD, Mayo Clinic, with Sandra Wendel)

Chewish: Stories of Love with Recipes from Nama's Kitchen

Chicken Soup for the Soul: Heart Disease
(compiled by Sandra Wendel)

Chicken Soup for the Soul: Breast Cancer
(compiled by Sandra Wendel)

Pitcairn's Island: A Book Report
(A+, sixth grade, Bryant Elementary, Sioux City, Iowa)

Catcher in the Rye: A Book Report
(C-, eighth grade, North Junior High School, Sioux City, Iowa)

COVER TO COVER
What First-Time Authors Need to Know about Editing
© 2021 Sandra Wendel, Write On, Inc.
(because 2020 was just too miserable to remember)

ISBN (paperback): 978-1-7326404-0-5
ISBN (ebook): 978-1-7326404-3-6
ISBN (audiobook): 978-1-7326404-4-3

World-class design team: Domini Dragoone, Miblart, Ada Vlajic

Published by Write On Ink Publishing,
dba Write On, Inc., a Nebraska corporation.

Contact the author at www.SandraWendel.com
Email: Sandra@SandraWendel.com
LinkedIn: Sandra Wendel
Twitter @SandraWendel
Facebook: FirstTimeAuthorsClub

To the many writers who write and
eventually become published authors.

Scribbled Verse
Upon a page
Memories in print.

The human mind—
A lone-ly thing
Written words our friend.

"WHY I WRITE" BY TOM LIGGETT

Call this section Contents, not Table of Contents, and there's your first insider secret.

Contents

Part I: I Just Wrote a Book: Now What?

**PART II: "I'm Ready for My Close-up, Mr. DeMille"
or How to Get Your Manuscript Ready for an Edit**

I Just Wrote a Book: Now What?

Part I

Chapter 1

Why Do I Need an Editor?

Ask not what your editor can do for you. Well, actually, that's the question you do want to ask when you're writing your book, feeling overwhelmed or stark naked actually about the whole writing and publishing process.

But wait, you say, *I need to find an editor. I'm a first-time author. I don't know how to do this, what do I do? I've never done this before.*

Exactly. You wrote your first book, so now what? You have questions like these:

- Where do I find an editor?
- How do I work with an editor?
- How am I going to publish my book?
- Hmm, is this book any good? Who'd want to buy it?
- I heard that I need to find an agent? Where do I find an agent?
- A friend told me I needed to have 70,000 words. Is that enough? Is 12,000 words too short?
- What does an edit cost?

- I need a copy edit and a proofreading, right? What's a developmental edit?
- I know the world is waiting for my book. How do I get it out there?
- I'm not a professional writer. How can I keep from making stupid mistakes in print?
- I read on the internet that ...

Am I right?

What This Book Is—and What It Is Not

This is the one book you need to read and follow if you're writing a book for the first time. Why? Because you've never written a book before. This is new territory.

To write a successful book, you need to find and work with an editor who shares your passion for your work and your message and who will help you make your book sing. And sing a smash hit. A blockbuster of a message, clearly and carefully constructed so readers love you and your work and leave you five-star Amazon reviews only because they don't have more stars to give.

This is a toolkit for tinkering under the hood of your working manuscript so you, the author, can take your work as far as you can before an edit and production such as cover design and not dump a half-baked chocolate cake on some poor schlub of an editor to "fix."

I will help you understand what editing is and what editors do and can't do. If you expect me, as editor, to write the next Pulitzer Prize–winning book for you, forget it. If I could write *that* book, my name would be on the front cover as the author. But it's not out of the realm of possibility that you can write an Amazon best seller. Many of my authors have.

I talk with new authors every day. I have also taught them in my classes on how to write a book at our community college for over a decade. I know you. I am you. I know your fears and your excitement. I know how you will feel once the doorbell rings and Amazon delivers a copy of your book to your doorstep and you rip open the padded envelope and hold your book in your hands for the first time. Let's take a three-second pause to savor this moment.

To get to that point, you must do your homework, and my goal is to walk you through the steps. Your goal is this: to write the best book you can and to produce it professionally and expertly.

You can make all the excuses you want: *This is the first time I've written a book* (we all had a first time). *I don't know how to do this* (so you bought this book, and I will show you). *I'm not a writer and other excuses* (that's what keeps us editors in business). *I don't know if this is any good* (I'll explain how the market determines that).

I am an editor of nonfiction. I even specialize in the areas of business/leadership, self-help/health, memoir, and true crime.

Even though my editing background is in nonfiction, the principles are easily applicable for fiction writing as well. And although I don't talk about character development, point of view, plot, head hopping, omniscient narrator, and structure for thrillers or romance or fantasy, much of the information here about how to work with an editor and fine-tune your manuscript will be helpful to you. Please consult some of the excellent books on writing fiction for the finer points of that craft.

This book is not a how-to-write-a-book book. However, in chapter 12 I offer some practical tips for how to move away from staring at a blank page to putting words on paper in a financially lucrative order. As much as I wanted to keep the focus of this book on editing, I conceded and included the information I present in my classes about writing, but it's just an overview.

This book tells you what to do next, after you have words on paper yet no plan going forward on what to do after that.

This book is not a manual for publishing, although I promote the independently published model—called author-publisher—and most of my authors are publishing independently. No longer a stigma to publish your own book, author as publisher is the most accepted way to publish a book because traditional publishing is broken and book agents can rot in hell (okay, I have issues with them and their scammy, scummy tactics).

I tell authors every day, "You can do anything any big New York publisher can do, and more, and should. Their model of selling through bookstores with agents as gatekeepers is broken. You are not Oprah, Michelle Obama, or John Grisham. The world is not waiting for you to write a tell-all book and buy a million copies the first day. Your book has a niche audience, so write it and find your readers and sell your book. You can swim in the same pond as any book with every book buyer, and that pond is called Amazon. That's where readers buy books. Not bookstores."

Yes, I'm sad that bookstores are struggling. The traditional publishing world didn't help them stay afloat, especially during COVID-19. But many worlds collided to change the way readers read (ebooks, audiobooks) and where readers get books (online). Those evolutions are coupled with the beauty and efficiency and low cost of digital printing for soft cover books, so I'd spend any gift cards you have for Barnes & Noble before it goes away. I present a lengthier discussion of the digital printing process elsewhere in this book.

I don't discuss marketing your book. That's a completely different world. BUT. And you knew there would be a *but*, the manuscript you create is the first step in writing a best-selling book that touches people's lives, enriches them with information, and must be coupled with a perfect title and subtitle and a professional cover and interior design to be taken seriously. And then you figure out how to sell it to the world. Plenty of book marketers will beg you to sit in on their webinars, take their Amazon Ad challenges, and optimize your book to find the book buyer. Listen to them.

This book is not about self-editing. I don't think you can edit your book yourself. I don't even edit my own books. My mentor is my editor, and she's tough. She finds the inelegant phrasing and fixes my twisted logic and pushes me to say what I want to say simply. She finds missing words, commas, misplaced modifiers, wrong words, and punctuation faux pas that authors don't have to pay attention to when writing and then completely miss when we revise and revise again.

Our brains are just wired to miss our own errors. My editor points out when I'm trying too hard to make a point (with a marginal comment and sometimes with revised wording that just makes sense). She tells me when I miss the point entirely or even when I run down into the rabbit hole of a complex sentence and can't find my way back home. She even checks facts when I misspell a name or place (not often, let the record show).

We editors are, in a way, the last line of verification for truth. Because once your book goes out into the world, you are judged by your readers, and they can be brutal. I'd rather have them engage me in Amazon reviews for true differences of opinion than point out a typo on page 165.

And that's what you want *your* editor to do. You have lost your objectivity at mile marker 10. Your editor brings that fresh set of eyes and knowledge of editing. Unless you plan to curl up with the *Chicago Manual of Style*, seventeenth edition, of 1,146 pages (that is not a typo), you won't know if *microorganism* is hyphenated or solid or whether to capitalize president of the United States or if Silicon Valley or third world are capitalized.

Again, that's what editors do. So relax.

This book is not going to teach you how to self-edit. But I offer a Checklist to help you look for issues and fix them well before you declare your manuscript ready for an edit. Nowhere else will you find such an extensive list of pet peeve words, sentence-level constructions to avoid, and just plain tips to make your words shine.

The Lesson from My Grandfather's Memoir

I frequently get calls out of the blue (if the blue means searching online) from people who have written a book.

"I'm a first-time author," they admit timidly on the phone as if that's an apology for something.

"I've been writing this book for four years," they tell me. "I think I'm finished."

I ask, "What's your book about?"

And then we go quickly down a long path of stammering and starting and uncertainty.

New authors don't give themselves enough credit. They feel compelled (and I'm told 80 percent of people have a book in them) to write a bunch of words on paper. Whether the universe is channeling through them or they are driven to get their thoughts down to save the world, document a career of service, or offer leadership advice for entrepreneurs, everyone has a reason for writing, and it's not my job as an editor to discourage them at all.

In fact, I feel that everyone should write their book or books. Write write write. Get it out. A purge or an exorcism or a divine presence guiding you. Get your book out. On the other hand, I don't think that every book that is written needs to be published, and I'll explain what being published means shortly.

My grandfather organized his memoir on 3 x 5 cards. He asked family members to give him their memories to be included. He outlined, and to jog his memory, he read a wealth of poems he had written for special occasions such as birthdays and anniversaries, and he sat down with yellow legal pads (he had plenty, he was still a practicing attorney well into his eighties) and in an elegant hand wrote his story.

I typed his words, page by page, chapter by chapter, on an IBM Selectric. We made copies on a copier, three-hole punched the 300 pages (typos and all, mine), and created twelve copies in three-inch-wide binders. Guess what everyone in the family got for Christmas in 1982?

He had a book in him. He got it out. And his grand-children and great-grands and great-great-grands are the beneficiaries today. His papers and his autobiography are archived at the University of Iowa in a special collection for accomplished Jewish citizens of Iowa. Is he a published author? No. So what?

Some stories, like my grandfather's, have a tightly lim-ited audience. Such a memoir today would exist on a flash drive containing all the family photos digitized and cap-tioned for posterity. Maybe even audio or video files of oral interviews. Even the manuscript would be in digital for-mat for safekeeping in a safe deposit box and passed down through the generations like our own Ancestry.com.

The Revolution That Changed the Way We Publish Books

If the book in you is ready to come out, you have a wealth of options today—more than my grandfather had. Because of the computer (the world's new Gutenberg printing press, which was one of the most revolutionary inventions for all humankind in the dissemination of information and learn-ing), because of digital printing (a process whereby books can be printed one at a time), and because of Amazon (the behemoth superstore, hate it or love it), books can be pub-lished and marketed and words can be read instantly in an ebook or audiobook or in a paperback delivered to your door in two days.

> That's the revolution in books that's
> changing the way we write books
> and produce them and sell them.

So if you're among the 80 percent of people with a book in them, we editors can help you create your family story, your bucket list book, your business card book, that novel and those characters that haunt your dreams, the poetry that magically flows from your fingers out onto paper, the book you always wanted to write.

Because writing books today and publishing them is so easy and simple and really quite low in cost, the bad news is that a lot of books are being published—a million a year. Even more bad news, many of those poorly written and amateurishly produced books are cluttering up Amazon, might sell a few copies, and languish on Amazon for years. The average independently published author sells about 300 copies. That's it.

These books don't sell for a number of reasons (take your pick):

- The authors **don't market** their books. The world will not beat a path to your door or your Amazon description page if you don't tell the world about your book. Marketing is difficult and can be expensive. Some authors stop at the publishing part. Sometimes that's okay.
- The books are **poorly written**. The marketplace determines whether a book is "good," and I discuss the value of "good" elsewhere in this book. A handful

of one-star or three-star reviews on Amazon can be the kiss of death for a book. Don't give your reader/ reviewers a reason to trash your book because it's poorly written (your editor can throw you a life jacket).

- Books are **poorly designed** and hard to read. When an author decides to save money and do the editing (or no editing at all) and design work themselves (I mean, how hard can it be to create a cover), it shows. Covers look homemade, with all the usual mistakes author designers make, like these:
  * Saying *by* author name on the cover is one. A big giveaway that this is amateur time.
  * Creating tight gutters on the pages meaning the words are bound too close to the spine (the gutter is well, the gutter, the space when you open a book, between the pages at the binding).
  * Choosing an unreadable sans serif font for body text (it's all about readability, baby).
  * Creating blocky titling on the cover and stock images without much thought to layout and design.
- A **terrible title** that doesn't tell a prospective book buyer what the book is about. There is a rhyme and reason to book titles, and new authors don't know the rules of that road. Many find out the hard way when a homemade cover (chosen because the author says, "I really love this photo") meets a pathetically simple title giving no clue as to the content of the book, and there is a recipe for disaster. Cover design and titling are an art and science. When you don't know what you're doing, when you don't rely on experts, it will show (in lack of sales).

- And my favorite: **poor editing**. Readers aren't stupid. They spot typos and story gaps and complex sentences. Lately, they are not shy about telling you so in scathing Amazon reviews. That's where I come in. I am an editor whose sole mission is to help you create a professional book that's easy to read and showcases your message, not your flaws.

These are just a few hallmarks of DIY book production. Readers know. But you're not an average author. You are ready to be a published author. A first-time author. And I am here to help you.

If you want to play in the book marketplace with a commercial-quality book, you need to know what it takes and hire professionals for the tasks you simply cannot and should not do yourself.

That's why you need an editor.

Chapter 2

What an Editor Does and Doesn't Do for You, the Vulnerable First-Time Author

Editors are the gatekeepers who help you revise and rewrite one more time to craft your best book possible. We polish the mechanics so you don't look foolish in print with misplaced modifiers, awkward commas, and misspellings, no matter what the nuns at St. Patrick's said about commas, they don't get typed in if you take a breath. We help "put the makeup on" so you are ready for a close-up when the time comes and you enter the publishing spotlight.

Contrary to popular belief, editors are not magicians. We cannot pull a best-selling book out of you. Only you can do that. I like to say I'm in the silk purse business. In other words, authors bring me pigs' ears and I try to make silk purses. Sometimes we can—together.

We editors work with what you bring us. A book coach can sometimes work with you from the beginning of your nugget of an idea for a book and help you land that plane. Editors are not book coaches. Oh, we do a lot of handholding along the way, and, yes, we coach from the sidelines, but we're not usually under the hood tinkering away as we rebuild an engine—although sometimes it feels as if we are.

I apologize for all the clichés in that last paragraph.

I wrote this book as a way to connect with prospective clients and current author clients. But I also want to use this book to explain my process and to explain the editing process in general—even if I am not privileged to be your editor.

Why Are You Writing a Book?

First, understand why you are writing your book. Are you checking off your book as a bucket list item or writing a family history or crafting a leadership book as a business card? Nonfiction authors are writing in various genres for various reasons like these:

TO TELL A STORY

Memoir: Used to be these types of books were referred to as *autobiography*, but *memoir* is a better term. Memoir encompasses a segment of a life (not birth to death, I mean, think about it). Memoir writers have a story to tell. A priest who worked with Mother (now Saint) Teresa in her leper colony in Yemen (Father Ken Vavrina in *Crossing Bridges*) has a story as well as does a Secret Service agent who guarded President Nixon years after Watergate during his renaissance in diplomacy (Michael Endicott's *After Watergate*). These stories are as much about people as they are a contribution to history.

I enjoy editing these stories, and every example I use in this book reflects an author, a real person, just like you or Judy Lund-Bell in her book *Flying with a Dragon on Our Tail* and her adventure flying with her husband in the historic Paris-Peking-Paris Air Race or Barbara Lynn Vannoy's *The 10 Greatest Gifts We Give Each Other*, a humorous look at marriage vows the second time around.

True Crime: Cops like to tell their street stories. Solving the haunting cold case. Often their families had no idea what they did while protecting the rest of us. Or a bank robber who has written two exposes about life on the street in a gang and then doing time in a tough California prison (Richard Stanley in *Up on Game*).

Cops, detectives, and air marshals don't need to watch *CSI* or *Law & Order* to find excitement in their storytelling. They lived it. Mark Langan's *Busting Bad Guys* series and Brian Bogdanoff's *Three Bodies Burning* will keep you up at night. Steve Fischer's *When the Mob Ran Vegas* will just keep you laughing.

Survival: Many memoirists have survived familial abuse, an abusive marriage, a delightful courtship, Satanic or domestic abuse or cancer or another dread disease or the Holocaust (the four Holocaust memoirs I have edited are special and dear to me, such an honor, such as Milton Kleinberg's *Bread or Death* and Lucy Lipiner in *Long Journey Home*). Lucy's description of playing with the frost on the window, as her only toy, while sequestered in Siberia remains among the touching passages that haunts me.

TO IMPART KNOWLEDGE

Business and Leadership: Not everyone is a Zig Ziglar or Simon Sinek writing the classic books that helped shape business. Although every businessperson wants to write *that* book or use their book as a springboard to a TED Talk, generally, business writers I work with have a formula to share and a lifetime of experience, advice, and lessons learned. They've been there and done that and want to write about it. Others use these books as a business card, an entrée to prospective clients, and a bonus as a speaker ("Introducing today's speaker, author of — ").

I've worked with CEOs (such as Gary Huff, former CEO of LabCorp and his book *So, Dad, How Did You Get to Be a CEO?*) and executive coaches (Dan Foxx who wrote *Confessions from the Heart of an Executive Coach*) and entrepreneurs and leaders of all types in many industries.

Health: I am an author too. Among a few other projects, I wrote two books with a third in the works with a doctor at the Mayo Clinic. He is the main author, and I am the "with" author, which means I do the heavy lifting with the writing, but the concepts and words and credentials are all his. Dr. Edward Creagan and I have written *How Not to Be My Patient* and *Farewell: Vital End-of-Life Questions with Candid Answers from a Leading Palliative and Hospice Physician.*

I spent my early career working at Boys Town with social scientists where I learned to summarize scientific studies for a consumer reader, so I like to think I can help authors explain difficult topics so you and I can understand them. I edit for mental health therapists and other health professionals as they write their books.

Of course, there are hundreds of other types of nonfiction such as history, spirituality, motivation, inspirational, art, technology, humor, and parenting, but I don't have as much experience in those areas and stick to the genres I know well. I can offer you guidance here, however, in how to find and work with an editor.

I have a bias. I think an editor needs to have some knowledge of the subject matter. I turn down work on books outside my area of expertise and comfort. I'll give you some tips on how to find the right editor and how to know a match when you see it in the next chapter.

Feeling Vulnerable? When Is Your Book Ready for an Editor?

I always cringe when someone calls or emails and says, "I wrote my book last weekend. I need an editor."

Yes, you do need an editor, but not yet. What you did was write a first rough draft. That's why I also cringe when I see webinars promoting "how to write your book in 30 days" or "write a best seller in six easy steps." You can't write a publish-worthy book in thirty days or in any easy steps. Writing takes time. Writing is rewriting, as so many successful authors say including my new boyfriend Stephen King, and nothing is that easy about writing.

But this book (which I wrote in several months with a career's worth of experience and many painful steps) is about how you can work with your editor once you have a working document.

So what does that working draft look like?

I like to tell authors, "Don't come to me until you are

sick of looking at your manuscript." "I want you to be completely done, not just tired of it." "I want you to have written and rewritten more than you ever thought you would."

If you feel you're at the point where you truly are sick of your working draft, please go over it with my Checklist at the end of this book and then contact an editor. You will find places to tighten, words to sharpen, redundancies to fix, and writing to revise.

Of course, some authors tinker forever, and I have to nudge them to let it go. They rethink and rewrite. They are always questioning whether this word is the perfect one or whether that scene is expressed exactly right. At some point, they need to stop. If that sounds like you, try this test. See if you can read at least ten pages without making a single change in a word or punctuation. If you can get through a random ten pages from the middle of your work, you're ready for an edit.

Also consider this. When you revise your work, are you starting at the beginning every time and moving through to the end and maybe you don't get through it all every pass? If so, your earlier chapters are going to have been reread and revised more than the latter half of the book. I see this all the time. Polished material at the beginning and half-baked chapters toward the end. Longer chapters at the beginning, shorter chapters in final sections.

If you insist on going over your material yet again, start in the middle. Revise your chapters starting from the back. Now wasn't that tip worth the price of this book?

When you first start drafting your work, let's say you wanted to look something up or hold a spot for more information, and you inserted something like this: [to come] or [check sp] or [find the reference] or [listen to the interview for actual quote here] or [???]. We old journalists used these markers to signal us to go back and fill in a detail so the writing process didn't slow us down.

If you left any sections blank or left markers, do fill in all those markers before you go into an edit. A detail left flying in the wind will remain that way until you make it happen. We editors have not mastered the art of mindreading, so be assured we'll flag you on that too.

Just to mention this rare occurrence, if you leave notes to your editor or yourself in the text, make sure you remove them. Sometimes the notes might look like [here is an example] part of the text but is really an editorial note and never gets removed. I haven't had an edit go to press with that type of error, but there's always a first time. Let's hope it's not in your book.

If you have specific questions for your editor, make a list of questions to submit with your manuscript or use the Comment feature in Word's Track Changes, which I discuss in more detail in Part II.

Your Editor Is Not Your High School English Teacher

Your editor is not (or should not be) a rigid tyrant. You are the author. Your name is on the front cover of your book. Your editor is a professional who can guide you in writing the best book you can.

We're also not your high school English teacher, so we will actually make editorial changes for you and leave you kind notes in the margin. We'll explain why you might consider different phrasing, and we'll suggest alternate words for you. We don't use red marking pens or keep you after school. We also don't grade you, and your graduation doesn't depend on your writing a sterling essay. Exhale now.

Your Editor Knows the Rules of Writing and Helps You Apply Them

Use our expertise to decide which level of editing your manuscript needs and follow a few smart steps to come to an agreement with your editor before any proverbial red pencils hit the paper:

DO THIS:

- Submit your entire manuscript to an editor. We need to see the entire beast, not just a sample (which is usually your first chapter, which is often the most rewritten).
- Let us evaluate the level of editing and decide whether your work requires a line edit or copy edit to move your work along toward publication.
- Ask an editor to perform a sample edit of, say, five pages or several hundred words. Then you can see the level of edit the editor is performing on your work. Let the editor choose where to draw that sample from (I randomly scroll and stop in the middle).
- Make sure the editor knows your goals for the edit. If you just want your words cleaned up, or if you're not open to making changes in structure or letting someone tinker with your words, then go with a copy edit. I explain the levels of editing in chapter 5, even though a copy edit may not be enough.

- Be open to editorial suggestions but know that you have the final say.
- Know when you want to break the rules. Editors should be open to capitalizing key phrases in your industry, even when *Chicago* style would not suggest caps. For example, when I edited *When the Mob Ran Vegas*, the author and I agreed that we would capitalize *Mob* and *Mobster*. We did. Consistently. That's the key. If you break the rules, be consistent.

DON'T DO THIS:

- Editors cannot be expected to write best sellers. If we could, I'd write one with my name on the front cover. An edit will help you put your best work forward. I call it getting the mustard stains out of the blouse or tie, so they're not distracting.
- Don't ask the editor, "Is this good?" Here's what I tell authors I work with: I can tell you if I enjoyed your story or the history or memoir or leadership advice. I am one person and I may not be your target reader. I can give you my opinion. If you want to test your work on the market of target readers, consider a beta reader process (discussed in chapter 10). I can make your manuscript mechanically sound and ready for publication. The goal of an edit is not to create the next Pulitzer Prize–winning work. It's to help you be as close to error-free as possible.

Once you and your prospective editor have had a speed date and feel comfortable working together, the rest of this book talks about how to get the most out of that relationship.

Chapter 3

Who Is an Editor and How to Find One

We editors are the nerdy students from your high school English class who loved to read. We always raised our hands and had the correct answers. We wrote our term papers with zest and turned them in on time. We aced the spelling tests.

You hated us.

We were the kids who read books under the covers with flashlights when our parents told us to turn out the damn light and go to bed. We lived vicariously through reading. We used our library cards and always had an armful of books.

We are those people.

Although I'm not a crossword puzzle addict, some editors are. They are deadly in word games, and you want them to be your "call a friend" if you get on a TV game show.

Nobody has a degree in editing although many fine universities offer certificate courses in editing. Some membership organizations, such as the EFA, ACES, or NAIWE, offer coursework in editing.

Anybody can say they are an editor, but only some of us make editing our day jobs. When I finally left the nonprofit world and opened my editorial services company officially in 1999, I had been editing on the side for academic presses and social science researchers. I had weathered my share of doctoral dissertations and formatting lengthy reference sections without poking my eyes out.

Editing is a skill that sharpens over time, with experience. I like to work with eager young editors because I learn from them too. We can comb through a manuscript and find grammar points to pick (and we do).

Some of us specialize in specific genres. I avoid editing fiction, but I'm damn good at many nonfiction genres. Chances are you've never known an editor. So how can you find one when you need an editor?

Can your next-door neighbor, a retired English teacher, be your editor?

No. That's the short answer.

I am indebted to my favorite high school English teacher, Miss Barker. I wonder if she really had a first name. But correcting your lame eleventh-grade essays is not the same as editing a book.

Book editors use the *Chicago Manual of Style*, the bible of the book publishing industry, for guidance on everything from what to capitalize to whether a comma goes before a restrictive clause, to how to set up a bulleted list, to which numbers to spell out, to what goes in italics.

Your English teacher will not know *Chicago* style. And I have had to follow along after an English teacher had her hands on a book manuscript and reinsert the serial comma (yes, *Chicago* uses the serial comma). They don't know the conventions for parts of a book or whether a Preface is really a Foreword or the style for bibliographic entries.

And that English lit major who is a friend of your daughter's? Not an editor. Or the novelist in your writing critique group? Probably not, but make these people part of your beta reading team (more on that later in this book).

I have a completely vested interest in convincing you that you do need a professional editor with experience in editing books in your genre. I rest my case.

No, there is no Angie's List of editors. I always ask my authors how they found me. And I asked myself how I would find me. Here are my best tips:

- **Membership organizations** for editors have listings and profiles. You can comb through the profiles at the Editorial Freelancers Association (www.the-efa. org) and look for a suitable editor who has experience in the type of book you are writing. Or you can post a job and an email is sent to EFA members. You'll receive responses to sort through. Other membership organizations are ACES, NAIWE, and Editcetera.
- Look in **books** you think are well written. See if the authors thank their editors in the Acknowledgments section. If the book was independently published, you might identify the name of an editor and then find that person online. If a book was published by a major publisher, the editors who are thanked are generally in-house editors and not available to you.
- I have a profile on **Reedsy** (www.Reedsy.com), which is an online collective of publishing services freelancers. You look through profiles of editors,

cover designers, and other publishing industry providers and invite a handful to quote your editing project. You've heard of other collectives of freelancers such as 99Designs, Fiverr, and UpWork. My only caution is that you identify editors to interview who are in the US. My bias is showing, but I would want a native American English speaker, not someone in the UK or Canada. Once you identify the name of a prospective editor, then Google the name and see if the editor has their own website, like I do. There you can review their credentials in more detail.

- Ask your **writers' group**, whether you meet online or in person, if fellow authors know suitable editors for you. I love referrals from other authors.
- Your independent **bookstore** owners and librarians may know local editors.
- A **Google** search for book editors will pop up a host of companies that specialize in editing. You can view their websites, read the profiles of their editors, and often see their pricing schedules. (But first, please read the next bullet.)
- Many **publishing services companies** (and I'm not talking about companies that bill themselves as publishers, per se) offer editing services. Beware of so-called publishers because many of them are in business to sell you services, up-sell you even more services, and sell you your own book. They offer publishing packages that include editing. I have worked for one of these companies, and I quit when I discovered they were up-selling authors (I recommended a low level of edit; they told the author that their book

needed a higher level of edit). That's fraud. That's a scam. Beware. Always Google the word *fraud* or *scam* with the name of the prospective publishing company to find out their reputation. Preditors and Editors at https://pred-ed.com/ tracks publishing scams. Victoria Strauss's Writer Beware® blog and website tracks these low-life publishing scammers well (https://www.sfwa. org/other-resources/for-authors/writer-beware/).

- **LinkedIn** offers a ProFinder service. You may have to be a paid member of LinkedIn to tap into this service, however.

A few words of caution: There is no watchdog group or credentialing organization for editors. Be guided by (1) books like yours the editor has edited; (2) references from other authors and give them a call or email and ask how their experience was; (3) a sample edit; and (4) a speed date phone call and gut check.

What If You Want to Work with an Editor in Person?

One author, in a post to find an editor, was insistent that the editor he chose would fly to his location, in California, two different times, block a few days to meet in person, and I wondered why. Writing is a solitary endeavor. So is editing. Not much gets done when the author and editor are hashing over word choices. I can see talking out a story line or organization of a book, big issues, but I just don't see hours of in-person time as being productive. Maybe for book coaching, but editing is not book coaching.

With Track Changes and the marginal Comment feature in Word documents, the author and editor can have a lovely and lively conversation in the margin of the working manuscript without getting bogged down about commas and exclamation marks. Why would you question the professionalism of your editor (the one you searched for, consulted references, and interviewed)?

But if you would prefer to find an editor where you live, I can tell you you'll have much better luck in California and New York (especially New York), because that's where most editors live. Unless you are in Omaha, and then you and I can have coffee together and tour bookstores and libraries to look at cover designs. But in-person meetings with an editor are not necessary.

Most of my clients are elsewhere (because I am in Nebraska). We have never had any issues or problems because we can't get together in person.

One caution: Please consider working with a US-based editor who is a native American English speaker. Our language is so damn hard to learn anyway, it's equally difficult for someone learning English as an additional language. I am also going to piss off my editorial colleagues in Canada and the UK and Australia. Sorry, mates, you don't speak American English, and you should not be editing books written for and distributed by American English authors for US readers.

Just recently I worked with an author based in Ontario. Our collaboration was a good match because his book was to be distributed via Amazon.com to US readers and Amazon.ca (Canada's Amazon platform). He elected to convert his spellings and usages to American English, so I changed *colour* to *color* and *honour* to *honor*. Those are easy. But he talked about vacation cottages on the lakes in Ontario. American writers would say vacation cabins or vacation resorts. These are subtle distinctions but critically important.

If you must meet in person somehow, consider Zoom. Frankly, if you make me wash my hair for a Zoom meeting, I may not be too happy, but it's doable. However, in an editorial meeting, we can accomplish much by looking at a document together, at the same time (Google Docs is ideal for this), and having a phone conversation as well.

Fair warning. Many editors are shy. They'd rather have you email them (1) so they have a record of the interaction especially if you are making changes by phone (don't do that), and (2) they tend to be nonconfrontational especially if you are talking about money, fees, payments, and cost for services.

What to Do When an Editor Steps over the Line (or under the Line)

I'm sorry to report that an editor can step over the editorial line. Twice in my editing career, I have batted clean-up for authors who had been working with an editor who completely rewrote their work. I mean rewrote. Every sentence. Wait, what?

Actually, the question is why. Why would an editor rewrite perfectly fine sentences? I'll tell you. I don't know these editors, but I suspect they have a self-importance that they are always right. Perhaps they fancy themselves as writers first and editors second and want to flex their writing skills. Just because they would recast a sentence in their words, they should not do that with yours. If your book is so poorly written, it should not be in an edit; you should be working with a book coach.

I respect the words an author has chosen, unless, of course, the words are incorrectly used. But I don't gratuitously rewrite sentences and entire paragraphs.

One editor even told the author that he wanted to become a coauthor because he had done so much developmental work. That tells me the author and editor did not have a firm understanding of what editorial work needed to be done going into the deal. Why would an author share authorship with someone who comes along after the concepting and writing and feels their contribution is worthy of authorship? Makes no sense.

The editorial service is just that: a professional service. Author and editor agree on the scope of the work, and the work is performed as work for hire. This is a critical distinction when it comes to filing for copyright. A formal filing for official copyright with the Library of Congress clearly spells out the name of the author or authors. Any other contributions to the manuscript (such as graphics or illustrations and editing) are considered work for hire with no stake in copyright ownership.

When an editor takes too many liberties and revises too much, the author's voice is lost (or at least changed) along with meaning in some cases.

But what happens when an editor doesn't do enough editing—or edits poorly? Again, I have been the second editor called in to reedit for some of these situations. More than I care to think about. How sad for a first-time author or any author to place their "baby" in the hands of someone they think is capable and move into production with a manuscript filled with editorial error.

Anybody can call themselves an editor. There is no college degree, but there are some excellent certification programs and courses, as I said. Many editors do internships for university presses and mainstream publishers. Editing, in a way, is an apprenticeship. Be careful about taking the low-ball editing price from a new, hungry editor who seems too good to be true.

What Happens When an Edit Goes Bad?

Twice just this year, book designers I know have contacted me and said, "Sandy, I am doing this cover and interior, and I think this book really needs an edit. I know [the author] had an edit done, but I'm seeing issues."

So I am called in to be like the circus roustabout and follow the elephants with my broom and sawdust. I do like to rescue a poor edit, but I also don't think it's fair to authors to think they have been well served and then find out it will cost them more money and time to get their work where it should have been.

In this case, I gently offer to do a close edit on about five pages in the middle of the manuscript and even a quick skim read and point out areas I see that need editing. In these runs, I find misspelled names (never fact checked), inconsistent punctuation (serial comma not used consistently or missing commas in independent clauses separated by a conjunction, not gray-area commas, for example). I see paragraphs that would run at least a page or more (and these make designers go bonkers) and inconsistent subheadings or photos without captions. Not to mention more serious issues with organization and chapter titling.

What if you're that author and your edit goes sideways?

First, make that designer your new best friend. They have saved you from the horrors of putting out a poorly edited book and the nightmare of one-star Amazon reviews.

Second, work with an editor who will not judge but just fix. You have to pay again for an edit.

Third, know that your book is that much stronger, more professional, and lightyears better than when you started.

As an editor, I know that we editors can quibble over style issues (which can easily be resolved by consulting our bible, the *Chicago Manual of Style*) and commas and organization. But when I find absolute error and inconsistency after an edit, well, those are unforgivable.

Sometimes the working manuscript in question just needs a thorough proofread while in Word document form (before it is created into pages as PDFs). Talk with editor #2 to see what you need and make it happen. (PDF stands for portable document format, and this step turns your Word document into actual book pages.)

Horror of horrors, your book is live on Amazon. You have ordered copies and sold some. And then some well-meaning person informs you of errors. If you deem those errors bad enough or wrong enough, fix your PDFs and reupload that new file. And see the discussion of absolute error under Proofreading in chapter 5.

No need to be embarrassed. Just fix and move on. Trying to get editor #1 to reimburse you is wasted energy.

By now you are wondering how to judge an editor's work, credentials, and pricing.

Questions to Ask an Editor You Are Interviewing

Pick up the phone and talk to someone you are going to entrust your precious manuscript to. Editing is an intimate process. You want to feel comfortable with the editor. My colleague Lisa Pelto of Concierge Publishing Services said, "When we edit, it's like going through your underwear drawer." It's as intimate as that.

Ask these questions and expect the types of answers I suggest.

What is your experience? Look for someone who has edited books like yours. If you're writing a true crime story, you may not want someone who specializes in romance, but it's possible an editor who edits mystery thrillers might be helpful. Ask about credentials, certifications from familiar organizations, coursework, length of time editing. At least a few years of experience would be optimal.

Can you give me three references of authors who have written books similar to mine that you edited? Call or email a few people the author recommends as references and ask how the process was for them regarding the editor's thoroughness, responsiveness, and ability to meet deadlines. If the editor has a website with books listed, try to find a few of those authors and make the same contact: "I see that Mary Jane edited your book. I'm looking for an editor and was hoping you could tell me how that experience worked for you."

Are you willing to do a sample edit? Ask the prospective editor if they would edit a sample of your manuscript. Let them choose the sample. I pluck a few pages from the middle. If you want to cross-compare the editing of a few editors, give them all the same five pages, for example. (And if you think you can get a free edit of your entire book by giving several editors different chapters, we're onto you.) If you get back a Word document with Track Changes and thoughtful marginal Comments, and if you think the editor found issues you had not considered but agree with, you may have found your match. Be careful of the editor who does unwarranted major rewriting.

Which areas of editing do you specialize in? An editor who has edited many books similar to yours, say memoir, can bring a wealth of experience to your edit too. You don't want to be the book a new editor experiments on.

What style do you use or recommend for my book? The right answer is, "I use *Chicago Manual of Style*, but if we deviate from that, in spellings or other conventions, I will keep you consistent."

What is the sequence of your editorial process? First-time authors don't know how the editing process unfolds. I explain that I like to do a two-pass edit process. In other words, I do a major first pass for everything the manuscript needs: content, sentence-level, mechanical such as punctuation. I know I will miss items as the pages start to fill with tracking and comments. But the first pass is intended to pick up most of the editing. Then the manuscript goes to the author for review, acceptance of the edits, and attention to the comments. At that point, the author may revise areas, add or delete sections in response to the comments, and respond to questions from the editor.

The manuscript then comes back to me for cleaning up, removing comments the author responded to, and another full editing pass. A few straggling questions may remain and can be ironed out between author and editor. Find out the process your prospective editor uses. Sometimes a one-pass edit for mechanical issues is all a manuscript needs. When you find that one, I'd like to do it.

How long will it take for you to start my edit, and when will the edit be completed? When you're ready to be edited and have checked off all the tasks on my Checklist at the back of this book, you don't want to have to wait three months for an editor to start your work. You're excited to get going.

Confirm a reasonable timetable with your editor: a date when you can deliver your final manuscript, the date the editor will return it to you for your review (a few weeks is reasonable to me; two months is not). You don't want to languish in a long line only to get bumped for someone with a more pressing deadline, even if you don't have a deadline.

You also don't want to be undergoing your edit while the editor is also juggling and editing four other manuscripts. (I promise my authors I only work on theirs exclusively when I begin their edit. I might throw in a load of laundry or mow the lawn for a break, but I'm not working on another distracting edit because each deserves my undivided attention.)

Do you do the actual work or do you have staff? If you are interviewing and possibly hiring Harry as your editor, you want Harry to perform your edit. Not a colleague he farms it out to or an apprentice who needs some practice. Unless, of course, you know someone else is doing the work and agree. Most editors are solopreneurs. I do have a bench of aspiring editors and colleagues I can call on for proofreading or copy editing, but my authors always know who has their hands on their work.

Do you read my entire manuscript before you price your editing? There's a misconception about having an editor read your manuscript before you even begin working together. We cannot and we will not. We want to stay naïve to the story so when we do start an edit, we can be your Every Reader, at least the first time through.

Will we editors look over your full manuscript? Yes, because we want to know what we're getting into and the best way to price the project. We know what we're looking for, just like your doctor knows how to diagnose you by looking at certain signs and symptoms. At least with an edit review, you don't have to take your clothes off.

Questions Your Prospective Editor May Ask You (and Should)

What is your goal in writing this book? If you are writing to make a million dollars, that goal is far different from the goal of writing a self-help book to help others. Editors will shy away from authors who want to write to become rich and famous because we know that goal may be unrealistic. Most authors say they want to document their experiences or teach others.

What is your book about? Give the editor your elevator speech (I *am writing a guide for entrepreneurs in start-up businesses. I just sold my own company and have a lot of wisdom to share.*), not a lengthy talk. The editor just wants to know the genre and your background. Why you are qualified to write this book. I stay away from authors who are not experts on the subject matter of their book. An example would be someone giving psychological advice to others about abuse or medical advice about a health condition, but their only qualification is their own experience. They are experts, of course, on their own story, but they are not qualified, in my view, to write advice for others.

What is your area of expertise? Editors want to know why you are the best person to write the book you have written. With memoir, that's easy. It's your story. With a business/leadership book, if you haven't been a manager or CEO or ever started a company, how can you be an expert on this subject? An editor can help you focus your platform and your expertise.

How do you plan to publish your book? Some authors have publishing contracts but still hire their own editors. In that case, I want to know what their publishing contract specifies in terms of number of words, focus, and deadline so we can hit those marks. Is there an in-house style guide? Author-publishers, on the other hand, need more guidance in terms of parts of the book, the process, and the shape of the final manuscript. We editors are filling in those gaps in knowledge for self-published authors.

Do you have a particular deadline? Editors can be booked out for weeks or months. If you have a pressing deadline or urgency in getting your manuscript turned around, the editor needs to know. If an editor is that good, is that editor worth waiting for? You have to decide. I try not to keep authors waiting more than a few weeks for a first major edit.

What type of editing do you think your manuscript needs, and what are you expecting from an edit? If you think you just need some commas fixed, and the editor sees a mess of paragraphs, no chapter structure, and numerous misspellings, just at a glance, then the conversation takes a different turn. A sample edit can clear up the mismatch between your expectations as an author and the actual editing your work needs.

Who is your target reader? Who will buy your book? Who should read your book? So if you say, "Everyone needs to read my book," we need to step back. I can't think of a book that everyone needs to read. Can you? Everyone is not your target audience. Readers fall into quite defined categories: romance, self-help, history, legal thrillers, memoir, business, health, parenting, and many more.

Your editor will help you define your target reader because that's the person you are writing the book to and for. P.S.: The target reader may not even be your book buyer. Consider gift books that are purchased by someone else for another person.

The bottom line is that your editor will help you speak directly to your reader. If the scope of your book is too broad, you'll miss the mark entirely and nobody will be your target reader.

How to Pay Your Editor

I would be foolish to quote pricing for editing. I discuss how editors price various levels of editing in the next chapter. Everybody has their own formula and price structure. I can only tell you what I do. Normally, I ask for half up front and half when you, the author, are delighted with my work.

Authors pay me with a check in the mail, Venmo, PayPal, Bitcoin (yes), or through a platform such as Reedsy, which acts as the middleman in the transaction and takes a percentage for setting up the "date."

Do We Need a Contract?

A contract? Some editors have elaborate contracts, which are about as useful as the emails I use for documentation, only more complicated and legal sounding. A simple contract can be useful. If something is going south, you'll be in a pissing match either way. Legally, you'll spend more than you'll recover if you sue an editor for poor quality work. Emotionally, the process can take a toll. Move on. Leave poor reviews if the offending editor has profiles on online sites and you have been truly wronged.

Make sure you document your terms in an email, even if the editor does not (about type of edit, dates and deadlines, promises, payments transmitted). Do you want to pay in full up front? Maybe not.

Having payment due as your leverage over an editor is the same as the editor holding up your final edited file awaiting payment. If you've had a lovely relationship throughout the process, payment and delivery are never a problem.

If, however, you are disappointed at the first editing pass, for example, or if the editor seems to be too slow and not meeting agreed-upon deadlines, then negotiate a kill fee (perhaps what you paid in advance) and move on. A kill fee is an agreement to end the arrangement, and the editor gets a small fee for work to date. Nobody is ever happy here.

One author thought she was buying a coaching buddy in contracting for my editing services. She wanted to write and revise and never finish her work (and there are reasons why, because she felt vulnerable and wanted to delay her memoir). When the author and editor figure out this delay tactic, negotiate a graceful exit for everybody.

I have seen other edits go poorly when an editor becomes overzealous and rewrites in their own style and words. As an author, don't let an editor change your voice, as I have discussed earlier. Editors don't rewrite (unless you pay them to and know that's what you're getting). You are the author. Stick to your story. A sample edit can reveal an obsessive editor before you get too far down the road. If so, reread the previous paragraph on a kill fee.

What if an editor doesn't deliver a well-edited manuscript? What if the editor doesn't edit enough? Of course, *enough* would be a matter of opinion, but if you were expecting some sentence revisions and just got a few commas here and there, reread the previous paragraph on a kill fee.

Here is the perfect spot for a summary of the author/editor relationship. Rest assured, most edits go well. Author and editor become best friends and live happily ever after.

Chapter 4

What Does
Editing Cost?

When an author asks about pricing, please consider that I (or an editor you are working with) bring a wealth of experience and knowledge and have refined and honed my editing skills, and that's what you are buying. All we can sell you is our time and expertise.

Some editors price by the word or the hour or by the page. I price by the project. I give a manuscript the level of edit it needs, no matter what we call it (I explain the levels of edit in the next chapter).

Let's look at pricing by the word. How can this make sense? An academic text with complex topics and explanations can hardly be compared word for word with a young adult novel. I think some editors and editing companies just quote prices per word because it seems efficient.

But what about pricing by the hour? Again, this process makes no sense. How long does it take me, an experienced editor, to edit your book? You should not care. In fact, an experienced editor may be faster than a new editor who stops to look up usage and style points. Are you getting a fifty-minute hour or a full sixty minutes? And how can an author possibly project how many hours an editor will spend on editing when the editor has no idea either?

We can edit a few pages and then extrapolate the time, but that's just an estimate. So I advise authors not to give an editor a blank check on number of hours. Or care if an editor is a $100/hour editor or a $20/hour editor. If you contract with an editor to pay by the hour, set a cap at ten or twenty hours and see where you are, if you really want to pay this way.

So let's charge per page. Okay, how many pages do you have? Your 70,000-word history of the world manuscript has 190 pages in a Word document. Oh, wait, is that single or double spaced? What font? What size font? Margins? All these variables determine "a page." Terrible idea to pay by the page. Some editors and editing companies say a random page is 250 words.

Stop playing number games with words and get a firm project price with an editor. Then you know the cost of your edit, and the burden is on the editor to deliver, within that price and still make a profit. Or at least cover an average hourly rate, which editors can privately determine themselves based on their experience, expertise, and cost to run their companies.

What If I'm on a Tight Budget?

Who's not on a tight budget? If you're going to be the author-publisher, you want to develop a complete budget for your book that includes editing, design, production, and marketing.

Although that budget is beyond the scope of this book, when I'm pressed to name a figure to publish a book, I toss out the amount of $5,000. Then the tire kickers who think they can get up on Amazon with their million-dollar book idea by spending a couple hundred bucks will know they're not a contender. Oh, they can get up on Amazon for a couple hundred bucks, but their book may look and feel amateurish without a professional touch.

And then I say, "If you have any money left over from your five grand, spend that on marketing." I could be underestimating that cost, but you get the idea.

As you explore the various professionals you need to call in to help you publish your book, look at industry averages for the various tasks. If you arbitrarily say your publishing budget is $1,500, then you'll have to compromise everywhere. Editing and design are not the places to compromise.

Shop around for pricing. Make sure you are comparing expertise and skills equally. If two equally qualified editors (based on experience, their references, work they have done, ability to meet your deadline, and a sample edit) are quoting you $1,800 and $2,800 for a line edit of your 60,000-word memoir, then price would indeed be the deciding factor in your decision. It's never that simple.

Nothing is more discouraging for me, as an editor, when an author says, "I have budgeted $500 for my edit." I politely decline to work with them and wish them well. Working with an editor is not like buying a used car. I rarely negotiate price or lower my standards or level of edit based on an author's budget.

Some authors think they can crowdsource their edit. Guy Kawasaki prided himself on putting out his manuscript for *APE: Author, Publisher, Entrepreneur—How to Publish a Book* (published in 2012 and now quite outdated) to his social media followers for editing. His plan was to have them get an early read of his book, recruit them to provide feedback on content and commas, sort through hundreds of responses, fix all the typos, and get himself published, and invite them to leave Amazon reviews—all without paying for an edit. How do you think that went?

Even editors don't always agree on commas and content, so imagine the CF he created from his early-reader feedback, and much of it had to be garbage and opinion.

No free lunch with editing. I refer you back to chapter 2, in case you skipped it, where I discuss who is an editor (not an English teacher you know or the legal admin in the office or your Facebook friends).

Chapter 5

The Levels of Writing and Editing Explained Once and for All (and If You Believe That, I Have Swampland for You in Florida)

The editing process is like any other professional service you contract for. An editor is often an independent contractor, a freelancer, who is a solopreneur, a work-at-home expert, or someone in a consortium of editors or a subcontractor for a publishing services company.

I started my editing company in 1999 after spending two decades in the nonprofit world working for the famous Boys Town where I worked closely with social scientists on their publications. I linked up with academic presses and began editing for them when editing was precomputer and

notes to the author were made directly on printed manuscript pages. For longer notes to the author, we applied
(pre–3M Post-It Notes) glued papers and wrote marginal
notes there. The process was messy. The working document
was sent through the mail and looked like your worst nightmare markup from your high school English teacher.

Consider this: The author had to read and agree with
my editing or leave a note, and then someone else had to
retype the manuscript pages with the edits and get all that
done correctly.

For another decade I worked with a national nonprofit
corporate wellness organization and developed materials for
incentive campaigns, handled press releases, and wrote the
definitive book on corporate health for a major publisher.

Computers changed everything, and now editing is
extremely efficient when done online in a Word document
or Google Doc. Marginal notes really are in the margin.
And all kinds of software can help find lurking issues with
writing style and just plain error. So when I began doing
freelance work, I bought my first IBM computer with two
floppy drives and learned Word Perfect. Today my iPhone
is infinitely more powerful than that $5,000 computer I
worked with.

Among my first major clients were MayoClinic.com
and eMedicine.com (later WebMD) where I wrote consumer health information and began editing books for
subcontractors for Amazon's CreateSpace (today's KDP,
Amazon's publishing platform). I also evaluated and
edited books for one of the largest publishers that has now
been discredited as being a scam, so I won't name them.
Suffice to say, I stopped working for them because of their

ethics when I discovered they were upselling their authors on unneeded services.

My take-home lesson was that I wanted to work directly with authors. First-time authors need handholding and guidance. When they freely admit they've never written a book before and are scared about the process, that's when I feel my services are most valuable. I walk them through, step by step, the editing, the revisions, and, for some, the production and a bit of marketing (I do admit marketing is not my strong suit, but I share experiences).

In my work with MayoClinic.com, I met Dr. Edward Creagan. He was a source they gave me for a story I was writing. Although I don't recall what story I interviewed him for, in the interview, he said, "I've always wanted to write a book."

If I had a dollar for everyone who has said that to me and a million dollars for everyone who says so but never writes that book, I'd be Jeff Bezos. But my dear friend Dr. Ed truly had a book in him, and together we collaborated on a book we called *How Not to Be My Patient*. Because he's a cancer doc, the title fit. I shopped it to publishers and found a home for the book with HCI, at that time the publishers of the Chicken Soup brand.

Although the experience was enlightening, the book publishing world was evolving, and we eventually got our publishing rights back. Dr. Ed and I formed our own publishing company (the publisher of this book) and revised *How Not to Be My Patient* and brought out the second edition ourselves.

We added a book on end-of-life issues because Dr. Ed is a palliative and hospice specialist, too, and *Farewell:*

Vital End-of-Life Questions with Candid Answers is another award-winning book. We have a third edition of *How Not to Be My Patient* coming out once the world settles down and we can bring updated information to the empowered patient in the new world of telemedicine.

When I found my precious grandmother's handwritten recipes, I knew I had to write a cookbook to honor her. I did. It's titled *Chewish: 36 Recipes of Love with Stories from Nama's Kitchen*, and although it's not anywhere near an Amazon best seller, I love to reread it for the family stories and I often make the recipes (my comfort food).

You see how I worked in my story here, in a chapter devoted to editing?

If you visit an auto dealer in person or online, you would be asked a series of questions starting with "What are you looking for?" You then decide if you want a van or an SUV, or what model or year, used or new, color, front-wheel drive, foreign or domestic.

Same with editing. Your editor should ask, "What are you looking for?" And depending on your expectations and what your manuscript actually needs (a combination of wants and needs), I can determine what level of editing is required to reach a goal (a polished manuscript ready for production) and how much time (mine) and money (yours) it will take to get there.

I'm not hedging my answer, but I really am. Like your new car, you won't know it's right until you see it. And with your manuscript, I won't know what it needs until I see it. Not a sample chapter. Not the Introduction, which is the section you've rewritten more than the rest of the manuscript. Not a summary.

I ask prospective author clients to show me the entire body of work. I've done this enough so I know what to look for, and which is why I wrote this book, so your working manuscript can be as far along and as polished as you can get it.

Why? Because then your edit will start at a much higher level than starting with the basics of making sense of tangled complex sentences or fixing misspelled words or moving chapters around to streamline the structure or writing subheadings.

You'll see various names for different levels of writing and editing. Let's start at the deepest level and move up from there.

Book Coaching

Some authors like to have a task master help them vision their book, make an outline, and use the editorial red pencil whip to keep them on task and writing. I have coached a few authors through the process, but the sequence takes months and even a year or more. This type of service is best priced at an hourly rate, contrary to what I said earlier about not pricing editing by the hour. This isn't really editing. It's coaching, like a personal trainer, only you don't do pushups. Set an hourly rate with expectations and caps on number of hours.

Collaborative Writing

Collaborating on the writing of a book can take many forms. I'll discuss the most common:

Coauthorship: When two or more people collaborate to write a book, they are each considered coauthors. The authorship relationship should be spelled out in writing in a legal document because inevitably something will go sideways. Decide who is the first author (John Smith and Joe Brown) and not necessarily in alphabetical order. The editorial challenge here is that with two authors, no one can write and use first person (They can't say: "When I was in graduate school, I took a course in psychology.") because the reader doesn't know who the I speaker is. This is a huge editorial decision, and I find myself untangling these types of arrangements all the time.

Most of the time, there is a main author, the person who wrote most of the book. We often end up dropping the second name. If the book is truly a collaboration, like Talia and Allen Wagner in *Married Roommates*, two authors I worked with who are husband and wife family therapists, they used we/our throughout with no problem.

Yes, there are ways to separate out individual experiences in first person, such as using indented stories with the name of the speaker clearly identified, or saying, "When I (John) was in graduate school" and so on.

With Authorship: When you see a book with authorship noted like mine: Edward T. Creagan, MD, *with* Sandra Wendel, chances are the first author is the main author, a solo author who can use first person throughout. The *with* author is someone who has contributed so much to the collaboration, the authorship spot is a gift, as Dr. Ed did so graciously for me. He thanks me profusely in the Acknowledgments and Introduction. Sometimes the *with* author is a ghostwriter who has been elevated to authorship status. You see this sometimes in celebrity memoirs or scientific books (the *with* author might be a talented science writer for the expert source who is first author).

Ghostwriting: Authors hire writers to write their books. This arrangement is called ghostwriting. There's nothing spooky about it. The writer brings the craft of writing, and the author brings the story. You often hear of ghostwriters for celebrity memoirs. In many of these arrangements (most are private), the ghostwriter interviews the celebrity author and crafts the book around a series of transcribed hours and hours of conversation.

Ghostwriters are paid well to do their "work for hire" and have no stake in authorship or copyright but may get some stake in royalties. I have ghosted a few self-help/medical books, but the expert authors dumped tons of material on me, so I was doing background research and shaping narrative from the author's talks and presentations. Drafts of these manuscripts go back and forth several times.

The most well-known ghostwriter these days is Tony Schwartz who was paid to write *Trump: The Art of the Deal* with Donald Trump, and Schwartz received *with* author status too.

Developmental Editing

Editors spend hours in workshop sessions and webinars discussing what a developmental edit is. I've taken courses on the topic too. Developmental editing for nonfiction and fiction can be quite different. Developmental in fiction may mean long discussions between author and editor about character development or how to fix holes in plots or where to break chapters for cliffhangers or even the point of view (who knows what when). I love reading a juicy legal thriller, but I won't edit them (too complicated with timelines and characters).

In nonfiction, developmental editing (to me) is taking that 35,000-foot view of the overall work and making sure the topic is covered in depth (medical and self-help books especially), by an expert in the field, with logical and progressive development of the points (business books, for example). Has the author answered the "what's new" about this book question? Are the chapters readable and do they flow logically? Has the author written at a level and with substance for the target reader? What areas can be cut? Or expanded? What questions remain unanswered?

Some editors read a manuscript just to deal with the content issues. In those cases, I hope the editors have content-specific knowledge. I don't profess to have that type of content-specific knowledge on everything. Instead, I try to be "the reader" and ask all the questions an informed reader might ask. That's the beauty of my not being an expert on any subject matter.

In a memoir, for example, as the reader I might want to know what happened to Aunt Patricia or why did the family move from Toledo or why is there a ten-year time gap between college and career.

Is a developmental editor going to flag complex sentences or is the editor going to revise them? This is a big deal. Ask the editor you work with to be specific (not just say in a marginal note, "I don't understand this," but specifically say, "I'm confused about whether Susan studied in Europe or finished her degree in the US, can you fill in this gap?"). Which note would be most helpful to you as author as you revise? Demand that level of attention if you work with an editor on developmental issues.

Scott Norton's book *Developmental Editing* talks about the DE as big picture, structural. He shows how to outline a book so author and editor can stand back and assess the direction and flow. He also said that some DE editors get their hands dirty down to the sentence level. And that's where you need to know what you're contracting for when you talk about your work with an editor.

I have seen developmental edits in which the editor acts more like a reader/reviewer, and there is no tracking, no tinkering at the sentence level, no fixes for style or punctuation. These edits are mostly marginal notes commenting on the narrative, much like an English teacher in a high school essay. I personally don't feel these types of edits are helpful to authors.

If you as author just want that overview read, then work with a developmental editor and make sure your expectations match what the editor is proposing to do. You can even ask for a sample chapter (but that's almost useless because the developmental edit is supposed to look at the body of work). Understand whether you are *also* getting a close edit, because you will eventually need one.

Sometimes developmental edits are also referred to as content edits or substantive edits where editors do intricate editing at the sentence level. Again, the editor would need some background and expertise in the subject matter to be useful. Don't send me emails if you disagree, because I know many editors will.

If you want someone to comment on your content, you need to find target readers and first readers to give you their opinions. Please review my discussion of beta readers toward the end of this book for enlightenment on this process.

Editorial Evaluation or Assessment

When an author says to me, "I don't know what level of edit I need." or "I'm not sure this manuscript is ready for an edit. What's missing?" or "Do you think this book has an audience?" then I offer an editorial evaluation instead of a developmental edit.

You may find editors who perform assessments. That's the world I'm most comfortable in because I can assess a manuscript without having the subject-matter background that a thorough developmental edit would take.

My manuscript evaluation (or assessment) is an overview. It is not an edit. I look at the big picture and the commercial viability of the manuscript when competing in the Amazon marketplace for readers/book buyers and whether the manuscript has all the relevant parts and pieces a book needs and how well executed the work is at that point.

When I am finished, I hope my assessment gives the author some direction to make any major revisions and certainly minor revisions, to view the prospective book in relation to the market and readership, and to give the author specifics about what to beef up, delete, and reconsider. Specifically, I look at many of these areas:

- Story line or arc or through line (memoirs clearly have a story arc)

- Character development (most often attributed to fiction, but nonfiction, especially memoir is often written in scenes with dialogue and character description)
- Setting
- Narrative flow and style
- Plot structure/scene development (in memoir, an essential part of the unfolding)
- Point of view
- Organization
- Pacing
- Format
- Accuracy of facts
- Clarity
- Tone
- Voice
- Dialogue
- Book title and chapter titles
- Suitability for intended audience and marketability (competing books)

The author receives a written report that covers the relevant areas. I also go through the manuscript, and using Track Changes in Word, I leave marginal comments as I skim read. I point out many of these elements and make suggestions.

I assume the author will be making major edits, but I also stop about halfway through and do a close line edit on about three to five pages so the author can see what a line edit looks like and the mechanical and grammatical issues I would be editing.

If you contract with an editor for an evaluation, make sure you know the editor's process and what you will get in return.

Line Editing

That close edit I discussed as part of my manuscript evaluation is called a line edit. An editor examines every word and every sentence and every paragraph and every section and every chapter and the entirety of your written manuscript. Typos, wrong words, misspellings, double words, punctuation, run-on sentences, long paragraphs, subheadings, chapter titles, table of contents, author bios—everything is scrutinized, corrected, tracked, and commented on.

Facts are checked, name spellings of people and places are confirmed. This is the type of edit I perform most often (but if I see some big developmental issue such as structure or redundancy or missing pieces, I will mention the item in a marginal comment and we can discuss). Editors should use the *Chicago* style conventions unless you and the editor have decided to capitalize special terms consistently, for example, or use a different style guide.

WHAT TO EXPECT WITH A LINE EDIT

A line edit includes all the editing tasks on my checklist for a copy edit plus a deeper sentence-level look at these additional fixes:

- Conduct heavier fact checking (for example, exact titles of movies in italics, death date of a famous person in history, the protagonist was using an iPhone before they were invented).
- Make suggestions about moving or removing text (or actually doing the task and explaining in a marginal note why).

- Initiate a discussion about why the dreary Introduction could be cut.
- Offer a new scheme for moving a chapter or two around to better accommodate a time line. (Actually doing the moving and writing transitions might fall into the category of developmental edit or left to the author to do.)
- Query the author in a marginal note about why Susan in chapter 2 was wearing a winter coat when the scene takes place in summer. Or whether the author intended for the detective described earlier with a full beard to be scratching his stubble.
- Point out repetition and inconsistencies in the story line. But not rewriting.
- Actually revise awkward sentences, break up long sentences, streamline sentences with clauses and parentheticals. Recast sentences that begin with *There are* and *It is*. Those constructions are simply not strong. That's why line editing is considered a sentence-level type of edit.
- Substitute stronger words for the commonly overused words (*very, pretty, things, great,* and *good* are my pet peeves).

Let me show you what an edit can do. This is a paragraph from Chris Meyer's book *Life in 20 Lessons*. Chris is a funeral home director.

A line edit would turn this rough paragraph—

> The more regular are the things that make life so cruel and unfair: a healthy man has a

> heart attack on his bike ride, a child stricken
> with cancer, a mother dying before her chil-
> dren reach middle school, a father on vacation
> with his children, a son abalone fishing because
> it brings him joy, a daughter in an auto wreck
> with her best girlfriends, a simple slip and fall,
> gunshots, the list is as endless as it is tragic.

—into this:

> More likely are the events surrounding death
> that make life so cruel and unfair: a healthy
> man has a heart attack on his bike ride; a child
> is stricken with leukemia; a mother dies before
> her children reach middle school; a father suf-
> fers a fatal stroke while on vacation with his
> children; a son drowns while abalone fishing;
> a daughter is killed instantly in an auto wreck
> with her best girlfriends; a simple slip and fall,
> gunshots, the list is as endless as it is tragic.

Copy Editing

When an author says, "I just want a copy edit," I ask what they mean. Again, there is confusion about what a copy edit includes.

Most of the time, authors want that thorough line edit. If a manuscript is so clean, so squeaky clean, so perfectly written with lovely paragraphing and fine-tuned punctuation, then maybe the manuscript just needs a copy edit. Like never. I can't even recall a manuscript that has come to me this clean that it would need just one pass for a polish for mechanical issues. Never. Not even books written by professional writers. And not even this book. I hired out my line editing, and it's a humbling process.

So let's just agree that when someone says copy edit, they really mean a much deeper and more thorough edit than putting commas in the right place.

WHAT TO EXPECT WITH A COPY EDIT

A copy edit is the lowest level of edit. Rarely does a manuscript need "just" a copy edit. Sometimes a copy edit is a final step performed separately by your editor or someone else with fresh eyes. Some editors (like me) do copy editing all along looking for these types of errors, and a copy edit is part of the line edit.

Here's my simple checklist:

- Correct any typos, which would include misspelled words.
- Fill in missing words.
- Format the manuscript before production, and that includes just one space between sentences (I don't care what you learned in typing class in high school, the double space messes up the document when it is converted into real book pages).
- Streamline punctuation and properly use commas, periods, and em dashes—like this. Avoid overuse of ellipses to denote a break in thought … when they are really used to show missing text. And those exclamation marks! I allow authors about five in each manuscript. Overuse them, and they lose their punch.
- Make sure the names of characters and places are spelled consistently throughout (Peterson in chapter 1 may or may not be the same Petersen in chapter 6).
- Find and replace similarly sounding words with far

different meanings (affect/effect, their/there, and its/it's are commonly mistaken).

- Conduct a modest fact check (perform a Google search to find the exact spelling of Katharine Hepburn or the capital of Mongolia). This isn't *Jeopardy!*, so you do get to consult resources. I keep a window open to Google just for such searches.
- Make new paragraphs to break up long passages.
- Question the use of song lyrics and remind the author to get written permission.
- Point out, in academic work, that footnote 6 does not have a reference source in the citations.
- Remove overuse of quotation marks. For emphasis, use *italics*, but sparingly. Books generally do not use **boldface**.
- Impose a consistent style for the text (this means using a style guide for capitalization and hyphenation, treatment of numbers, heading levels). *The Chicago Manual of Style* is preferred unless the work needs to conform to an academic convention such as APA, AMA, or MLA.

Let's Clear Up the Blurry Line between Line Editing and Copy Editing

Editors disagree about many of the finer points of their work such as whether to capitalize the word *president* (no, generally, but yes with *President Lincoln*), whether to spell out numbers (some styles say yes to every number lower than 10 or lower than 100), or whether to use the serial comma that preceded this clause (*Chicago Manual of Style* says yes).

Editors also disagree about whether to start a sentence with *And*.

And of course editors disagree about what constitutes the levels of editing that are often labeled copy editing, line editing, substantive editing, and developmental editing—or just simply editing.

In editing world, we editors do agree that your manuscript deserves a professional and sound edit to make it free of typical errors of spelling and punctuation, with proper use of the right word, judicial paragraphing, logical chapter breaks and chapter titles, and prudent fact checking for accuracy—and, above all, consistency.

As Random House copy chief Benjamin Dreyer said in his exceptionally fascinating book, *Dreyer's English*, "My job is to lay my hands on that piece of writing and make it … better. Cleaner. Clearer. More efficient. Not to rewrite it … but to burnish and polish it and make it the best possible version of itself that it can be."

For guidance, I turned to the authority, the *Chicago* manual. Yet even that widely accepted all-knowing guide doesn't make a distinction among editing levels: "Manuscript editing, also called copy editing or line editing, requires attention to every word and mark of punctuation in a manuscript, a thorough knowledge of the style to be followed, and the ability to make quick, logical, and defensible decisions."

For reference, and for those of us editors who can geek out on anything related to a comma, see chapter 2 (Manuscript Preparation, Manuscript Editing, and Proofreading) in the *Chicago Manual of Style* some night when you can't get to sleep.

Then we consider why edit at all? Because readers are better able to enjoy your novel's characters and follow the plot or a memoir's poignant scenes instead of getting hung up on obviously misspelled words and clunky punctuation. A few Amazon reviews that say "needed an editor" or "should have used spellcheck" can be the kiss of death for your book's success.

New authors are often confused about what level of editing they need, and rightly so. I hope these sections have given you some insight into the process itself. So let's now get right down to word level.

Proofreading

Let's say your manuscript is fully edited (no matter which level you chose, sometimes even a developmental followed by a line edit with the same or different (preferred) editors). Your work will need a proofread either now or after it is designed in pages.

I prefer to hire proofreaders to proof for absolute error when the manuscript is in final pages or PDFs. But you can also proofread before it goes into production (and into PDFs), just knowing that you do need another proofing of the PDFs.

Use a different person, a different editor, even someone who is a professional proofreader. This person brings a fresh set of eyes to the work and scours for absolute error such as name misspellings, wrong URLs, bad URLs, numbers that don't add up in a table, double words, missing words, and those crazy stupid errors you as the author have missed and your editor missed, and you question your sanity. Those errors.

A proofreader doing the proofing at the PDF stage will look for all these types of errors plus others: bad word breaks and hyphenation at the end of a line, hyphen stacks (many words hyphenated at the ends of lines, stacked), widows and orphans (single words or lines at the top or bottom of a page), wrong captions with photos, page numbering, missing and misspelled headers and footers, page numbering matches with the table of contents, lines too tight or too loose. Many of these production issues are introduced as pages are created.

Again, I prefer to spend the time and money proofing in PDFs.

Proofreading is not the time to revise, rewrite, and delete. Your interior page designer might actually kill you. At the very least, major changes in proofing in PDFs can be time intensive and expensive. Put in the work way before you see your baby in actual page layouts.

Should you proofread your own work? The short answer is later, if you're in writing mode. The shorter answer is never.

Why? Because it's your work. And your brain plays funny tricks on you. It will fill in your words, and you'll be completely shocked when a professional editor returns your edited manuscript. *What? How could I miss that?*

Most editors won't admit this, but we, too, miss things. We're human (or many of us are). The errors I hate the most are those I introduce into someone else's writing. I have no excuse for that.

So the question on the table is when to proofread. Go ahead and edit and revise and rewrite all you wish and need to (and you need to). Yet I cringe when my authors say, "I need to give this one more proofreading."

Then they read their manuscript out loud or backward and hope to catch more issues. Generally, not a good idea at all because we skip words when we read aloud too. But I have heard of some authors having their computer read to them using the Read Aloud feature in Word.

I tried it out (click Help on your nav bar and ask how to use it). It was like *Star Wars* where C-3PO was reading unemotionally to me. Freaky, but the droid didn't skip any words.

Best advice: hire a professional to edit and another professional (that other set of eyes, and not just your mother-in-law who loves to read, but welcome her feedback on absolute error only; ignore anything else she says) to give your final manuscript a proofread for the dumb stuff everybody else missed.

A Final Word about the Process of the Edit

My method is to often conduct a two-step (sometimes three-step) edit, as I have mentioned. Here is the sequence:

1. First major editing pass for everything from typos and punctuation to flagging areas that seem confusing. I fact check and fix word by word, sentence by sentence. The document looks messy. I have included some examples in this book of how Track Changes looks (next chapter, but wait there's more). Marginal notes using the Comment feature become a dialogue with the author. I ask questions. I point out items. I encourage examples or dialogue or expansion. Or I ask if this or that can be deleted.

2. The manuscript goes to the author who reviews the edits, accepts or rejects, and responds to the marginal comments.

3. My second major editing pass cleans up the author's responses to the comments and any new material the author adds. I conduct another full editing pass, but at this point the manuscript has moved much closer to being final. During this pass, I can fine-tune sentence structure, note phrasing I may have overlooked during the first pass, and overall sharpen up the flow.

4. The author reviews new tracking in this document and cleans up any lingering marginal questions.

5. I resolve everything, accept any new changes and edits, and declare the work is ready for cover and interior design.

If only the process worked that smoothly. After a first major pass, authors rethink. They revise. They write another 3,000-word chapter. They start doubting their ability. They worry the book is not ready for prime time. They feel naked and vulnerable. They want to get outside validation.

Like talking someone off a ledge, I talk authors through the process, allay their fears, and we work toward creating a final published book.

I've talked about the levels of editing, but why not see what that looks like in the next chapter.

Chapter 6

How Does
Editing Work?

Seeing is seeing. In this chapter I'm going to show you screen captures of actual manuscript editing (with thanks to my authors for giving permission to share).

But first, a brief discussion of Word's Track Changes. If you already know how to use this editing feature in your Word program (Word on a PC and Word for Mac, not .pages), skip to the next section.

Open a Word document. Track Changes can be found here, depending on the version of Word you are using (and, fair warning, all this navigation can change with new software updates):

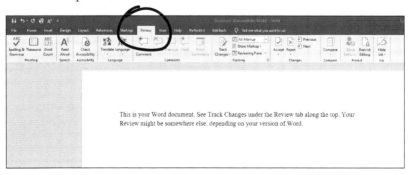

Click on **Review,** and you see this navigation with **Track Changes.**

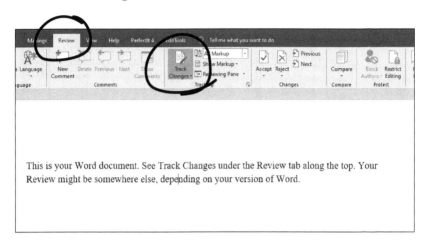

This is your Word document. See Track Changes under the Review tab along the top. Your Review might be somewhere else, depending on your version of Word.

Click on **Track Changes,** and the box will turn to gray so you know tracking is on. You can also see **Track Changes: On** at the bottom left of your screen too. I also clicked the box next to **Track Changes,** and the dropdown shows I have clicked on **All Markup.**

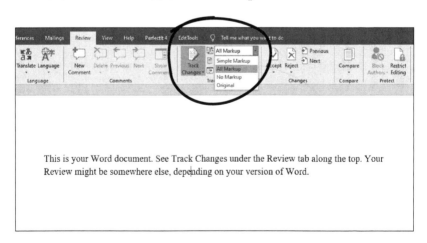

This is your Word document. See Track Changes under the Review tab along the top. Your Review might be somewhere else, depending on your version of Word.

This is not a comprehensive tutorial. Please search YouTube for plenty of videos that walk you through Track Changes especially if you're using Word for Mac (I use PC). For our purposes, just know that any keystroke you make in the document now will be highlighted in a different color.

Write your book with Track Changes **off**.

When I edit, I will turn tracking on, and you should keep it on. We ping-pong the manuscript back and forth, and we each can see what the other person has done. Word assigns each writer/reviewer a **different color** (which you will not be able to see on this black-and-white page unless you're reading the ebook version) and marks your marginal Comments with your name.

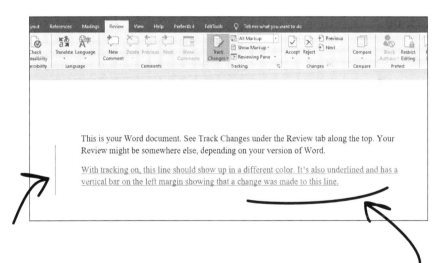

By clicking on **New Comment,** the program creates the marginal box where you can have a conversation with your editor. Note the **Reply** feature inside the marginal box.

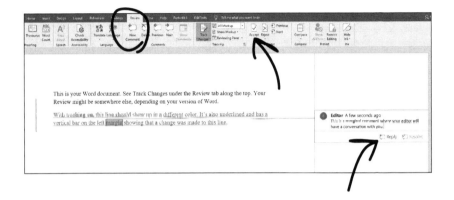

Now you have the basics. The best way to learn to navigate Track Changes is to open a document with text that you don't care about (in case you mess up). Play with all the features. Turn them on and off, click on the dropdown box choices and see how the screens change. Highlight a change and click **Accept.** I know it won't take you long to realize the power of Track Changes and how this process has revolutionized editing.

I am not going to discuss changes in Google Docs, which is a second-choice option and not as powerful as Word's Track Changes. Editors agree, so far, that Word is the superior editing engine, and documents created using Google Docs can be downloaded in Word for editing. Again, YouTube videos can be your best friend.

Above all, save save save. Always save early and often when you are writing. And save while you are editing (yes, I know, Word does a periodic save, too, but if you're subject to flash power surges and have ever lost an hour's worth of work, you'll File/Save).

My favorite story about saving is my dear author Rita Rae Roxx who wrote her stunning book *Once Upon a Rock Star* on a Mac, seated on her bed, starting in and typing 60,000 words. One paragraph. She never saved. She never printed. She never put the file on a flash drive. Lucky.

What Editing Looks Like IRL

In real life, editing looks like this. I thank my author friend Mark Langan for allowing me to show you actual screens from his manuscript, our editing, our notes, and the final product, his book, *More Busting Bad Guys: True Crime Stories of Cocaine, Cockfights, and Cold-Blooded Killers.* (I know, right? I'll wait here while you go to Amazon and order your copy.)

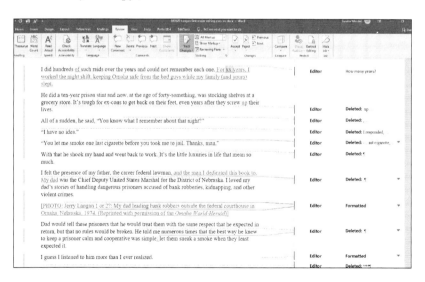

This is another shot from Langan's book. I show you this page because I'm going to show you its evolution. You're looking at a page in his original manuscript with my first major editing pass.

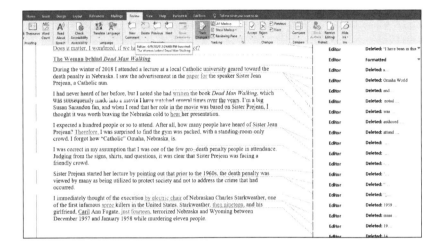

The second version shows all the tracking accepted. The colors and markings go away. Once the author approves this version of the manuscript, it goes into production.

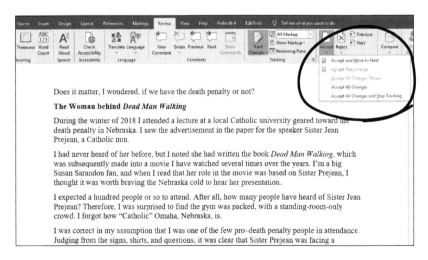

A book interior designer works with the author to create the look of the page: the font, the size, the spacing between lines, the font treatment for subheadings, the headers (book title, author's name, or chapter title), the placement of the headers and footers (page numbering), the margins. This is that same manuscript page only in a PDF—the actual book page.

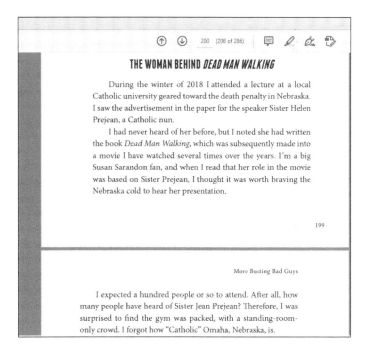

And this is the actual printed book page, in the book:

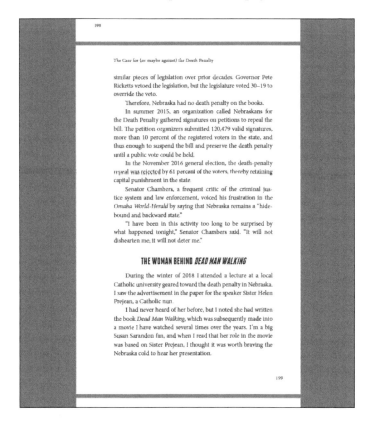

If you spotted the typo that crept into the final book, congratulations. The lesson is this: even final book pages are not always final. Errors can be fixed, PDFs revised, and new files uploaded to KDP.

Let me end this chapter with a caution about version control. Sounds ominous, but it's just that only one working draft of your manuscript should exist at any one time. You create your working draft, and let's name that document something like this: 022521YourBookdraft.docx. I use a date format. In this case, February 25, 2021 expressed as 02 25 21. It's actually quite efficient.

When your draft goes to your editor, the editor might rename the file: 031221YourBooksw.docx. I add my initials and update the date.

Do not tinker with your manuscript while your working draft (shall we call it the football?) is out to the editor. Take that time to give your brain a break from your work because you are too close to your manuscript.

If you have a bright idea about adding something, keep a list. When the football is back in your possession, then you make those changes. To keep the sports analogy going, you ping-pong the draft, and only one person can make changes at a time. Do not email the editor with a minor word change here or a new paragraph there. Those changes never happen the way they should, and your editor will consider murder as an option.

Hands off, if it isn't your turn. Imagine the mess trying to cross-match among drafts? Been there and it isn't pretty.

When I have a final file that is appropriately edited, has been back and forth between author and editor, with all issues resolved, all tracking and marginal comments accepted and deleted, then I name the file like this: 061421YourBookFINALforproduction.docx.

That is the end goal. How do we get there?

Chapter 7

Typos and Errors and Wrong Facts, Oh, Crap!

"I found a typo," the author says.

"Oh, crap," I reply. This is not the discussion I want to have with any author.

Here's the evolution of the editing error I showed in the last chapter in Mark Langan's book *More Busting Bad Guys*. We had worked closely to organize the chapters, and I had done two major editing passes. This after he and his wife, Annette, had read and reread the chapters many times.

He told the story about Sister Helen Prejean, the *Dead Man Walking* nun who doesn't look at all like Susan Sarandon who played her in the movie. His chapter was about the death penalty. He heard Sister Helen speak at a local event. My proofreader found "Sister Jean Prejean" and marked it for fixing in the page proofs. Fixed!

Or so we thought. Dang. There was yet another instance of *Jean* instead of *Helen*, and all four us missed it multiple times. Why? Because we're human. We make mistakes, and then we get too close to the material and our brains fill in what we expect to see.

Happily, Mark somehow saw the mistake or a friend saw it, and he texted me the offending page. I wanted to throw up. These aren't mistakes we editors want to make. His book had not gone live on Amazon, and the mistake was easily corrected, and a new interior file was uploaded to Amazon. Done and done. Until Mark (or his eagle-eyed readers) point out something else.

Did the world end because of that error? No. Will most readers see that error? No. Was the error a material breach of fact? No. An absolute error? Yes.

But what happens when there is an error that makes a difference? Thomas Edison is quoted as saying something about people dying from a typo. And here's the quirky part of that. I could not verify with the Edison museum archivist if Edison said it at all, and that's a lesson about fact checking for another chapter. Suffice to say, if you have critical life/death facts in your book that could harm someone if they are incorrect, hire a fact checker and make sure you are correct.

The worst error of fact in any book I worked on was in *When the Mob Ran Vegas* by Steve Fischer. A Las Vegas historian, Fischer wrote charming stories about the characters that shaped Vegas history. Howard Hughes played a huge role (in case you didn't know), and myth and curiosity surrounded the billionaire who holed up in an entire floor of the Dunes (which he owned) for years. At one point, Hughes purchased a tract of land that was later to become prime real estate, and Fischer said this about Hughes:

> He did a nice thing for his elderly aunt, though.
> The Husite Property he had bought, the 27,000
> acres of desert that the jackrabbits even thought
> was too far out, just before he left Las Vegas,
> he decided to rename that acreage after his
> favorite great aunt, Amelia Summerlin.

A year or so after the book came out, another Vegas historian politely emailed Fischer to say that was not a reference to Hughes's aunt but to his grandmother. Again, an error of fact that could have and should have been known to Fischer and fact checked before publication. The world didn't end at that point either, and the error was corrected in the production file and reuploaded to Amazon, and subsequent printed editions are correct.

> He did a nice thing for his elderly grandmother,
> though. The Husite Property he had bought,
> the 27,000 acres of desert that the jackrabbits
> even thought was too far out, just before he left
> Las Vegas, he decided to rename that acreage
> after his grandmother, Amelia Summerlin.

Brain Tricks and Hidden Goofs

The photo I took at the McDonald's drive-through is simply to make a point. How many people do you think saw this window sticker before it was produced and sent to thousands of Mickey Ds across the country?

This type of error only affirms my response when authors say, "I don't need an editor."

I attended an author fair and chatted with at least forty authors (mostly aspiring, not rich or famous, but people who buckled down and wrote their dream books and generally used independent publishing means to put their words on paper for others to read). Bravo to them.

I took this photo at McDonald's. Can you spot the typo?

Sadly, some indie authors still think they really can do it all themselves. Yet the successful ones recognize that some parts of publishing are best left to professionals—namely, editing and design.

Just to put a point on this point: No, your neighbor's son who is majoring in English or the high school English teacher from your book club is not a book editor. No, your niece in design school who knows her way around InDesign software is not a cover designer. And, no, you cannot edit your own words.

One author at the fair told me she "proofed" her book manuscript thirty times. And then, she said, she read it backward (some think they can find errors by reading out loud). I followed an online forum in which authors discussed the best software to read their books to themselves, as if it would help them snag a stray typo.

As an experienced editor, I just shake my head in disbelief but am willing to be convinced.

Smart authors understand that a professional editor (experienced, somebody who has done this successfully for a long time) will find content flaws, develop better chapter titles, suggest places to cut and points to expand, and mechanically bring the manuscript up to professional publishing standards using the style guide of choice for books, the *Chicago Manual of Style*.

If you want to continue to do DIY editing, know that you may not always know whether to use *complimentary* or *complementary*, whether to use a comma before *which* (or is it *that*?) clauses, whether an ellipsis is better than an em dash, whether the period goes inside or outside the quotation marks, or whether, for example, the red dress in chapter 2 was changed to a blue dress in chapter 6.

You can read your work thirty times or out loud, but you'll never know what you missed until those cruel Amazon reviewers pick your work apart, and those reviews just don't go away and can be the kiss of death for your cherished book ("Could have used a sound edit." "OMG so many wrong commas.").

We editors don't get everything right or perfect, but we can get you much closer than you can get yourself, no matter how many times you think you have "proofed" or read backward or read aloud to your cat.

You owe it to your work to make it shine, and for that you need to call in the pros for your prose.

Typos. They're like germs. Lurking where you least expect them. But are they really tiny errors? An innocent misspelling on a sign like the McDonald's window sticker said, "When *your up*, we're up." When indeed they meant, "When you're up, we're up." I still chuckle about that one.

Did you spot the extra L in Colllege? Plenty of viewers did on national TV. And it made the tongue-in-cheek joke about Nebraska football (another sport we play here) seem

A major goof was seen on national TV.

so true: "What does the N on the football helmets stand for?" The answer is knowledge.

But let's talk about typos. The internet is filled with examples, so you only need to look, well, anywhere. Everywhere. Although no one wants to die of a typo, imagine a sloppy physician writing the wrong dosage. That truly could be life threatening.

My current typo story involves the post office. The mail person incorrectly input the zip code for a package I was mailing to Pocatello, Idaho. The reversed numbers took the package to Rawlings, Wyoming, in error. The post office bounced the mislabeled package back and forth between Denver and Cheyenne until someone, a real human, actually looked at the typed address and redirected the package to Idaho. Thank you.

Take your time, check your work, have someone else proofread important messages, and take ownership in being right, even if your words aren't plastered on McDonald's drive-through windows or spread across the top of a dugout during the College World Series.

An Error or Two Won't Kill You

In my writing classes, I make the case for editing by showing how Amazon reviews can make or break your book's success. Here is my slide:

1.0 out of 5 stars
Where was the editor for this book?

Dang, I wish I'd read reviews before wasting my money on this. I have to admit, I didn't even finish the book. In the first 5 chapters alone, I counted Jane Austen's name misspelled twice ... I stopped reading because of these annoying errors. Looking at other 1-star reviews, I see I didn't miss anything.

And this one—

2.0 out of 5 stars **Needs an editor**

I don't understand all the five stars. There are too many punctuation errors (especially with commas), use of apostrophes to form the plural of words, and word misuse (using the word glimpse when the author meant glance) in the book.

The worst part was inconsistencies in the story. The father doesn't drink before five o'clock, yet he had several drinks at his next lunch. The friend is pregnant but had lemon drop martinis at happy hour. The secretary managed to spread a rumor before she found out what the rumor was.

The story itself is only average in entertainment value. I agree with the reviewers who said the dialogue is good. But the narrative needs more work,

and the book is a bit too long. Not bad for a first
novel, I suppose, but the author should invest in a
good editor.

Okay, one more tragic kiss of death for a new author—

3.0 out of 5 stars **Needs an editor**

A professional editor could have helped craft this book
to tighten up the conversational tone.

1.0 out of 5 stars **One Star**

Not worth the $ or time.

Don't let this be your book.

Like my coffee mug says, I AM SILENTLY COR-
RECTING YOUR GRAMMAR. And if you ask my kids,
you know I correct them not so silently at the dinner table.

Errors of fact often show up in manuscripts and can be
easily checked, verified, double-checked, and corrected. I use
my friend Mr. Google. Of course Google is not the ultimate
source. Google (more precisely, we say *perform a Google
search*, not *googled*) is the gateway to the ultimate source.

Let's say I want to check the spelling of a medical procedure. I put *blepharoplasty* into a Google search and find a
source, such as Mayo Clinic or WebMD or a university medical center, and that's the source I would trust for spelling.

Wikipedia is not considered an authoritative source
except if you scroll to the bottom of the Wikipedia page on

your topic, you'll find links to what might be an authoritative primary source (books, respected journals, magazine articles, and interviews).

This part has taken us into the nitty gritty of an edit. Although I don't recommend that you become your own editor, you can prepare your manuscript for an edit. And the next part of this book goes in depth into how you can be your own editor to a point, even if you don't play one on TV because there are no editors on TV.

"I'm Ready for My Close-up, Mr. DeMille" or How to Get Your Manuscript Ready for an Edit

Part II

Chapter 8

How to Format Your Working Draft for Editing

So you think you have mastered the intricacies of the latest version of Word. You can impose styles and headings and spacing and do fancy stuff. You choose a variety of fonts for your chapter titles. Another funky font for subheadings. Boxes and colors and caps and small caps. Something really sophisticated for lists, and—

Stop. Don't.

Here's why. When the final draft of your pristine and perfectly edited manuscript is ready for production, the Word document is put through a meat grinder. Well not really a meat grinder, but designers use software called InDesign. All you need to know about InDesign is that it works magic, along with a talented designer, to create the pretty book pages you see. And it strips out all the formatting you played around with as you played book designer. (Note to self: you are not a book designer.)

For example, if you are reading this book as a paper-back, you will notice the headers (the book title at the lower left and the chapter title on the opposite page at right), the page numbers, the indents for paragraphs, the graph-ics sprinkled throughout, the styling of the fonts for the chapter titles and the subheadings and subsubheadings, and bulleted and numbered lists.

All those design features, including the actual font itself for these very words that constitute the body of the work and the spacing between these lines and the spacing around the entire page—all that is specified in the InDe-sign program. Which means any fancy formatting you do in your Word manuscript is lost. Gone.

The final file you get for uploading to KDP/Amazon's publishing platform is a PDF file. It's a page-by-page ver-sion of your book with the actual book pages, designed and ready to print, like this:

 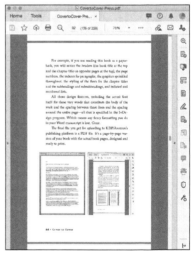

If you're reading this as an ebook, here's how that process works. The PDF file is somehow by magic and fairy dust that I don't know about turned into a different format called EPUB (the format you need for KDP). Think about the way you read an ebook. There is just text on your screen, whether it's an iPad, iPhone, other phone, or computer or Kindle or Nook. No headers, no page numbers, just scrolling text.

You can adjust the look of the page with contrast, reverse white on black, make the font bigger because you lost your reading glasses, and that flexibility is reflected in the EPUB files and why you see funky stuff like big white spaces before photos and other design features in books that are heavy on graphics, illustrations, and photos. That's ebook coding 101, and the extent of my knowledge.

And now is the curtain ready to come up? Are you really ready for your close-up, as Gloria Swanson, the aging movie star, asked director Cecil B. DeMille in my favorite movie of all time, *Sunset Boulevard*? Let's see.

When to Use *Italics* (some), **Boldface** (not a lot), and <u>Underlining</u> (never)

You can and should insert italics and boldface in your working manuscript where appropriate. Here's where:

Italics: Common words that should be in italics (which means the words will be shown in italics in your Word document and emerge in italics in your final book page) are book titles (*Gone with the Wind*), movie titles (*Gone with the Wind*), TV shows (*Orange Is the New Black*), paintings

(*Mona Lisa*), and tons of other terms. Whereas, song titles are expressed in quotation marks: "All You Need Is Love."

First-time authors tend to overuse italics for emphasis on words and then punctuate the sentence with an exclamation mark for, well, *emphasis*! I take out the italics and the exclamation marks when I edit. You really really have to make your case to keep those in. My philosophy is that the words themselves accent the importance, not the italics or punctuation.

Boldface: The *Chicago Manual of Style* isn't a fan of boldface. In fact, there aren't any or many uses for boldface suggested. However, if you want to use boldface, go ahead, but be sensible and sparing. I like it for words and phrases that introduce a bulleted list, for example.

Underline: Never use underlining in books. Oh, there I did. Sorry. I've never done that. Feels creepy.

Boxes and Sidebars

Some nonfiction books lend themselves to material that would be suited for a box. An aside or an explanation or a definition. If a section of your work should be treated differently, just mark it so in text and discuss how you would like the text to look (different font, indented, in a box) with your designer. Depending on how much material you have being treated typographically different and the design of your pages, let a talented designer make some suggestions.

In text I mark material to be handled differently with bracketed direction, like this: put [BOX] at the beginning of the material and [END BOX] at the end of the material. How easy is that?

In summary, just get the words right. Don't worry about what they look like. That's what we editors do in edit and what your designer will do in production.

How Long Should My Book Be?

Mark Twain is credited with saying something like, "I would have written you a shorter letter, but I didn't have time." Meaning: Write what you're going to write and then prune the hell out of it. Writing is rewriting, say all the savvy writers. It takes time. Part of writing and rewriting is tightening down and trimming to the bare bones.

We editors measure book length in words. Don't tell me how many pages you have cranked out because your Times New Roman 12-point font double-spaced might get 250 words per page and another person's Arial 10-point single-spaced pages may contain twice as many words.

Word software tells you exactly how many words you have (see the tab marked Review/Word Count, as one way to see word count). If you have turned on the word count feature, you can see your running count in the lower left corner of a Word document screen.

But I digress.

Many industry people throw out 60,000 words as book length. But as an editor, I've seen manuscripts come in with 200,000 words and some with as few as 6,000 words. The hedging answer to best length for a book is, "It depends." What is your genre? Who is your audience? What do you have to say? How detailed do you want to be with footnotes and end notes and indexes? Is your book an ebook only (shorter and longer books can sometimes be better in just ebook release).

To the author of the 200,000-word history of the Omaha Playhouse, I suggested making three books, a series. We ended up chopping to just 120,000 words (still lengthy). Extra material, background, additional photos, even lengthy notes and bibliographies can be taken out of the published manuscript to shorten it and moved to the book's website.

To the authors with fewer than 20,000 words, I often say keep writing. What more do you know?

And for those of you who skipped here to the end, the answer to the question, "How long should my book be?" is simply this: long enough and short enough to tell your story. Period.

Oops, Did You Add These Sections before Your Edit?

First-time authors often don't know about the various sections of a book they need to write. Here are some you may not know you needed (or don't need), and this is the order in which the sections usually appear:

PRAISE PAGES

People like to say nice things about your book. You just have to ask them. We call these blurbs or endorsements or testimonials. You see these on the front cover, like this one from my coauthored book *Farewell* from a well-respected physician who is recognized by his name alone:

> "Every human deserves dignity and peace in the final chapter of life ... a must-read book that could help those caring for the terminally ill." —Deepak Chopra, MD

You see these blurbs on the back covers too. And when you can get somebody who is well known to say something, anything, about you or your book, use it. My bank robber author, Richard Stanley, was honored to have comedian and podcaster Adam Carolla say this: "Richard Stanley is by far one of the most interesting people I've ever interviewed." Now that's pure gold.

And you see page after page of praise inside the front cover of many books. You can call this page What Readers Are Saying or Praise for [name of your book].

I encourage authors to invite people whose names are well known or who work for companies that are well known or people who are authors of familiar books. I don't know about you, but Oprah isn't in my Rolodex. However, dream big. If you want Oprah to endorse your book, find a contact for her and email an invitation. If you write a military history and want some five-star generals to read and endorse it, ask them. If your book was inspired by the author of another book, invite that author.

What's the worst that could happen? Oh, yah, they might say no. You might not hear from them. Okay, move on. Or they might email back and say, "Send your manuscript."

Most endorsers don't need the entire work. Offer to send the table of contents page and the Introduction and first chapter. Give them a realistic deadline. Move on without anyone who doesn't respond.

TITLE PAGE

List the complete title and subtitle of your book. The author's name (you). Your title if that's to be included, and the name of the publishing company you set up if you're doing an author-publisher model.

COPYRIGHT PAGE

Check any published book and you'll see a page printed at the left-hand side after a title page with a wealth of essential fine print. If you don't supply this information, your editor should prompt you for it:

- Year of copyright and the symbol © or word *copyright*
- Name of the copyright holder (that's you, the author)
- Publication information that includes the name of the publishing company and a contact email or website or both for the author
- ISBNs, and these are like VIN numbers for cars, you register your work and assign a number for each version such as paperback, ebook, and audiobook; buy them at www.myidentifiers.com in the name of your publishing company (the best deal is a bank of ten because you'll use three immediately and save the rest for your next book). Do not be tempted by free or low-cost ISBNs (then your book is identified in someone else's name).
- Disclaimer that says you are not responsible if the reader thinks you are giving medical or financial or psychological advice because you are not taking responsibility for their actions if they jump off a bridge or put all their money into cryptocurrency (either find

a sensible disclaimer in a similar book and use that or consult an intellectual property attorney to draft one for you), but be advised that people sue people for anything and everything, and a disclaimer isn't really much protection.

- Changing names, and this statement is often part of the disclaimer if you acknowledge that the story is true but you changed names of people to protect their privacy (and it might even prevent Uncle Ted from claiming you libeled him when you wrote about his sexual abuse when you were nine years old); however, there are much bigger issues of libel (that's saying bad things about people, even when they are true) that are beyond the scope of this book, so please talk with an attorney before publication if you feel someone will come after you if you tell the truth about them.

- Other information on the copyright page such as credits to people who gave you permission to publish their photos, for example.

DEDICATION

Dedications of the book go on a separate page. Keep them short and sweet if you use one at all. Save the longer thank-yous for the Acknowledgments section.

To Mother.

*To Harold who helped me
when I needed you the most.*

To my patients.

CONTENTS (NOT TABLE OF)

This is your road map for the reader. Unless you're writing something academic, you won't need an index, so the contents page (just call it Contents, not Table of Contents, amateur mistake) becomes your guide.

Make it as detailed as possible for readers. In ebooks, the chapters all link directly to the chapter pages in text too. That's why I encourage authors to make their chapter titles as interesting, captivating, and descriptive as possible. Would you rather see Chapter 9 or Chapter 9: Pet Peeves, Tigers, and Bugbears, Oh, My! Words Make the Difference?

Do not put page numbers in your contents page of the working manuscript. The actual page numbers are added by the interior designer when your book is in production.

FOREWORD

The Foreword is rare in nonfiction unless you get somebody famous to write a page or two introducing you. The Foreword is not about them. And if that person is that famous and wonderful, grab a quotable snippet and use that as an endorsement on the cover, or say on the cover, Foreword by BIG HOLLYWOOD MOVIE STAR.

Forget a Foreword. Move on. But note the spelling, which means a word that comes before (fore word, not *forward*, another amateur mistake).

PREFACE

I wish I had a dollar for every time I renamed a Preface an Introduction. What the hell is a Preface anyway?

INTRODUCTION

Now here is the part where you, the author, tell the reader why you wrote the book or any information you want your reader to know before you jump into the real meat of the book.

Sadly, some readers tell me they skip the Introduction and go right to chapter 1. I don't have an Introduction in this book for that very reason. People are busy. They like to skim. You have fifty pages to get their attention. And maybe not even that many pages before they leave the book in the hotel room or on the airplane seat. Get to it.

CHAPTERS, PARTS

Nonfiction books need chapters with titles (fiction books have chapters, numbered, no chapter titles). Number your chapters starting with 1 sequentially.

If your book is somewhat complex and falls nicely into chunks, or parts, call these big sections parts and number them with Roman numerals.

EPIGRAPHS

When Dr. Creagan and I wrote the first edition of *How Not to Be My Patient*, we included what we believed were thought-provoking chapter quotations. These are called epigraphs for those of you playing at home with the *New York Times* crossword puzzle.

For our chapter 5 on stress, we used this quote:

> All the resources we need are in the mind.
> —Theodore Roosevelt

Okay, fine. But eventually every darned book started using epigraphs for every chapter, and finally we have all heard every word uttered by Gandhi or about those journeys of a thousand miles. Enough. Epigraphs have become noise too. (Business book authors, take note.)

Yet, I have a solution. If you insist on quoting somebody, quote yourself. Quote your wisdom from that chapter.

In the second edition of our book, in chapter 5, we used this quote from Dr. Ed:

> Only one person truly cares about your health and welfare, and that's you.

See the difference?

RESOURCES/BIBLIOGRAPHY/ REFERENCES/NOTES

Depending on the type of book you are writing, you might include references for further reading. I have done that here. I know people reading this book might want to find other books on topics I have introduced. As the author, I am encouraging you to explore further. I also know that I have read these books, not just looked 'em up somewhere, and I wouldn't list a bunch of books just to list a bunch of books.

Business and self-help books often have Resources sections for further reading.

More academic books use an extensive Bibliography and Sources Cited or References where books and journal articles and online sources are detailed. In most consumer books, these types of listings are noise. No one reads them.

If you insist on citing sources, direct readers to the book's website where you can list them. Online sources often list a URL. Well, we know what happens with those URLs. They're impossible to type in from a paperback entry. They are never clicked on when hyperlinked in an ebook. I discourage authors from bogging down their books with references (of course, if yours is an academic book, don't listen to me) and broken hyperlinks.

An **Appendix** is that pesky organ nobody needs and usually flares up when you least want to hit the ER for an operation. An appendix is not what I recommend calling back matter or extras or bonus material authors tuck into the back of their books. Just give these sections a name, as I have done here with my BONUS: Checklist. If you want to keep an academic feel out of your book, don't use the word *appendix* or insert footnotes or have an extensive bibliography because readers will run for the hills.

And about **Notes**. A Notes section means the author may have inserted superscripts in the narrative to denote a footnote. I hate these. If you're writing for a consumer reader, do not use footnotes, especially footnotes that appear on the bottom of the page (nightmare for ebook readers), and your interior designer will send you chocolates if you don't have footnotes. If you need to note something as an aside or clarify, you have three options:

1. Work the reference into the text: "In a study at Johns Hopkins and published in the *Journal of the American Medical Association*, study subjects were …" You've given your reader enough of a clue to find the original source.

2. Gather the notes at the end of the chapter in a section called Notes to Chapter 5. Make reference to the item they clarify like this:

Regarding the number of books published, Publishers Weekly *said the number of books published each year is ...*

3. Gather all the notes in the book at the back in a section titled Notes and list them by chapter as in item 2 here.

Just a fair warning. If you are the expert, why are you citing hundreds of others in your book?

ACKNOWLEDGMENTS

Note the spelling of that section (no e as in *acknowledgements*). I often see it misspelled, and that's a clue the author didn't get a professional edit. The other clue is having the words *By Harrison Franklin* on the front cover (never use *by* on the cover or title page)—a real DIY no-no.

Authors often throw their acknowledgments together at the last minute, when it commands you spend time and attention. In the acknowledgments, thank everyone and anyone who helped you with the book.

- Family, always supportive no matter what
- Friends for remaining friends during your writing process
- Coworkers for putting up with your incessant talk about your book that is finally finished

- Your children for giving you time to isolate in the home office
- Your dog for warming your feet on those long, cold winter nights while you were creating your masterpiece
- Your computer geek who found the deleted files
- The UPS guy for knocking so hard on your door and scaring the crap out of you
- The squirrel outside your window who climbed into the bird feeder and gave you a needed humor break
- Your mentors
- Your yoga teacher, trainer, coach, psychiatrist, barista
- Your bridge club, the mah jongg girls, walking partners, and Facebook friends

But don't forget other key people who had a stake in your success:

- The librarians, name them, who helped you do research
- The archivists who found obscure materials
- The early reviewers, your beta readers, your online writing group
- Local bookstore owners
- Editors and production people, cover designer, proofreaders

People love to see their name in print. When you include names in your acknowledgments, you have created your little marketing team who will tell their friends through the amazing power of social media about your book, and you have your first marketing strategy checked off the list.

ABOUT THE AUTHOR

Here's where you shine. Don't be modest. Write your bio for this section and include a photo. A photo will be in black and white in a paperback but in color for your ebook.

A short bio is appropriate for the back cover—one or two well-crafted sentences that explain who you are.

Here's an example from *Mozart in the Garden: Silicon Valley and Me, We Grew Up Together*, a memoir by Tom Liggett:

From the back cover:

Tom Liggett is one of the world's foremost experts on roses. He founded the San Jose Heritage Rose Garden, the second largest public rose garden in the world. This is his third book.

And inside the book, here is Tom's longer bio (and I shortened it here to make a point about how the author bio is a marketing tool as well):

About the Author

Tom Liggett was conceived under an apricot tree and born in a brothel. His biological father, MT Liggett, liked innocent, dark-haired girls and pretty hookers. MT sired at least twenty-seven illegitimate children by as many women. He supported none of those mothers and just two of their children. MT only sent support to Tom's mother when the US military forced him to do so (or when they could catch him). This put Tom and his mother in dire straits. When he was a child, Tom was hungry and alone much of the time.

Tom was spawned in an orchard. He was taken into the orchard in a banana box when he was just two weeks old. His mother needed the work and refused to "waste" money on babysitters. When he was just a little older, Tom toddled around the orchards and fruit processing sheds. When Tom was three, he could identify the various stone fruit types.

Age eleven was a pivotal time in young Tom's life. He was an old hand at reading and interpreting college-level horticultural texts. That was when he began to accomplish rudimentary plant research projects in his suburban ghetto backyard. Tom also began to work. He needed money for food, toys, books, and music. Tom knew that hard work was the only avenue that led to eating regularly. ...

Tom worked as a boilermaker, electrician, car salesman, tree cutter, nurseryman, maintenance man, weed cutter, and farmer. Tom accomplished bench-level special chemistry projects for the Surgeon General of the Air Force.

In the midst of that occupational chaos, Tom managed to become Apple Computer employee number 114. Tom oversaw a staff of hundreds and had the only unlimited charge account in the company ("You never knew when I might have to get the manager of the local hardware store out of bed so I could buy some emergency supplies."). Tom had one of just twenty private offices at Apple, and, as Tom said, "That was good, because my office contained two full-sized couches. I didn't want to stop working long enough to go home for sleep."

Tom founded the San Jose Heritage Rose Garden, the second largest public rose garden in the world. He was chief rosarian for another major public rose garden. He has built and maintained countless private rose gardens. Tom has worked for many different nurseries. He has owned three successful nurseries and has three private gardens of his own.

He now grows plants only for his friends, family, and himself. He grows much of his own food. He also remembers what it was like to be hungry, so he grows tons of top-quality produce to feed the hungry. Tom operates the last, full-spectrum working farm in downtown San Jose. He doesn't sell anything, except during a couple of annual charity plant sales. Tom lives with his wife, dog, and gardens in San Jose, California.

Make sure your bio contains all the information your readers want to know about you especially if you are writing as an expert on a topic. Cast your bio in third person because you're talking about yourself. Think of this as writing an introduction to you that someone else would read if they were introducing you before you give a major speech. Ta-dah!

Back Cover Copy

Eventually you will have to write the content that goes on your back cover. So why not take a stab at it while you are writing your book. Stick to about 200 tightly written and carefully crafted words that summarize your book, the promise for the reader, the sizzle, and the completely shameless marketing pitch.

The back cover may be the most difficult part of your book to write.

Most authors don't even think about it or give the words much thought. Just the opposite. This is your elevator speech, and although you are not going to the top floor of the 163-floor Burj Khalifa, you are taking the elevator up a few floors.

Let's say you tell a friend you are writing a book. "Oh, what's it about?" the friend asks.

You say, [fill in this blank].

That's your elevator speech, and you'd better stop in thirty seconds. Play with those words, revise and revise.

Most often, the back cover copy becomes part of a longer Amazon description on your book's Amazon page.

You can also boil down your bio to two or three lines, as I did for Tom in the previous section.

Critical Pieces of the Book You Must Address

Captions: Every photo has a caption. Every graphic and illustration needs a caption unless they are decoration, but avoid gratuitous graphics. All photo credits are researched and credited. You may not take photos off the internet and use them.

Permissions: If you use somebody else's work or photo or illustration, you need written permission. Even if you use quotations from people long dead. You can try to paraphrase, but even summarizing Stephen Covey's seven habits of highly effective people may be a violation of the heart of his work. Forget about using anything from Disney or Seuss. Here's the test: why do you need to use anybody else's work when this is your book? (Yes, I know, history books are a different story. Archival photos in a history are essential. And sometimes you just need to quote something.) Poetry? Needs permission.

Song lyrics: You can't use them. You just can't. Not even one line. Don't even think about it. But you can mention the name of the song and the artist.

Grammar: If you want to play English teacher, consult a grammar text or online at https://www.grammarly.com/grammar-check where you can paste in some text for checking. I'm also a fan of the Grammar Girl (https://www.quickanddirtytips.com/grammar-girl (for blog posts and a podcast)). If you hated grammar in high school, you'll still hate looking up usage. Let your editor be your guide.

Spelling: Consult the high goddess of spelling, that's Merriam-Webster's unabridged at https://unabridged.merriam-webster.com/ (required paid subscription) or www.m-w.com. Try some of the spelling and usage quizzes on that website. They're fun. And distracting.

Spelling and grammar checkers: Don't be tempted to change a word's spelling or click "fix" in a grammar checker if the word in your text is highlighted or flagged. Spelling and grammar checkers are notoriously wrong, and AI has not yet replaced me as your editor. Especially don't trust the grammar checker. But if a word is flagged for spelling, on a final editing pass, go ahead and look it up.

Five reasons why you don't want to rely on spelling checkers

1. Online spelling checkers don't always catch mispelled words.
2. Checkers can be wrong. Its just their thing.

3. Don't you want to sharpen your writing skills anyway? Why rely on a computerized checking program. Your human.
4. Okay, I concede that sometimes a spelling checker does catch something I don't. But how often do typos and mistyped words crop up that aren't underlined in red or green or blue and are still wrong? The answer: lots of time.
5. Did you catch the typos in the previous four points? Thought so.

I rest my case.

Now you have all the parts and pieces of a book as you get your manuscript nearly ready for the editor to perform exorcism or professional magic.

Chapter 9

Pet Peeves, Tigers, and Bugbears, Oh, My! Words Make the Difference

I've never used the word *bugbear* in my writing, until now. It just shows how distracted you can get when trying to find synonyms for *peeves*. My pet peeve words are *things*, *great*, *good*, *pretty*, *very*, and *really*.

Think about the word *great*. What exactly does it mean? I'll wait—

For many authors, everything is great. The trip was great, the experience was great, his mother was a great woman, we watched a great sunset, and the friendship was the greatest ever. Have I made my point? Throw the word *good* in this category of nonwords too.

And *things*. Things are always looking up, the greatest thing (note the double ick factor here) about being a manager is this, and I'm going to throw up if I have to use that word one more time.

In just about every instance of using these pet peeve words, you can substitute a stronger, more descriptive word or revise the sentence to avoid using the word.

Some examples from real writing—

Before:

You can be a great executive without being a self-serving ass. You can be true to your values, highly professional, have integrity, care about others, and accomplish worthwhile goals while contributing positively to society and helping others in the process. I use these next chapters to help you on your journey to be a great executive the right way.

After:

You can be an exceptional executive without being a narcissistic and self-serving jerk. You can be true to your values, highly professional, have integrity, care about others, and accomplish worthwhile goals while contributing positively to society and helping others in the process. I use these next chapters to help you on your journey to be an excellent executive the right way.

(Gary Huff, author of *So, Dad, How Did You Get to Be a CEO?*)

Before:

We filed for 8,000 feet because of the strong headwinds. We were very tired.

After:

We filed for 8,000 feet because of the strong headwinds. We were exhausted.

(Judy Lund-Bell and Jim Bell, *Flying with a Dragon on Our Tail*)

And Then You Might
Use the Wrong Word

What's your favorite dessert? My fourth-grade grandson answered this question for his "about me" classroom project with "Mojave" as his favorite dessert. It has become an iconic family story. Max wants Mojave for dessert. Of course, Max confused two words: *dessert* (think ice cream) and *desert* (think cactus). One little s made all the difference in choosing the right word and getting the correct scrumptious delight as opposed to a prickly surprise.

Our family has developed an ice cream concoction we call Mojave dessert. And Max? He'll never forget how to spell the cactus or the cake. I'll bet you have a spelling word you stumbled on and vividly remember being mortified in a class spelling bee. Mine was *stomach*. I recall putting an e on the end, probably thinking about *stomach ache*, and blew a whole semester's worth of 100% perfect spelling scores with one measly little e.

The online dictionary can be your best friend here.

Or You Might Use the Same
Word Too Many Times

Which brings me to favorite words and pet peeves. When we write, we tend to use the same patterns of sentences, and we tend to choose the same words. Boring. That's what the thesaurus was invented for, and a simple right click on a word in Word drops down a box where one choice is synonyms. Remember this simple *mnemonic* (I always wanted to use that word somewhere, and it means reminder, prompt, or cue because I just right clicked it) about the *s* in synonym meaning same? Same words, similar meanings, those are synonyms.

Try this writing trick: Let's say you find yourself typing *amazing* in your sentences. The dinner was amazing. Her smile was amazing. And if you do a search (in Word, double click to highlight the word and then control F), the navigation will tell you how many times you used the word *amazing* and exactly where you used it. How many is too many? Switch things up. Just right click on the word and then click synonyms from the dropdown box and you get *astounding, astonishing, remarkable*, and more.

I think 1,476 exclamation marks is too many no matter how long the document. True story, I removed that many exclamation marks from one manuscript. I also think the word *things* used more than a dozen times in a book is too many.

Everybody uses the same words over and over when they write. And actually when they speak too. Think about how you describe a sunset. Spectacular. Unbelievable. Amazing. And the overused word *awesome*.

Your *awesome* and my *awesome* can be quite different *awesomes*, I would think. Maybe mine is streaks of blue and pink dashed across a serene Midwestern summer evening when the catfish are biting along with the mosquitoes. Your sunset might be the green flash just as the burning orange summer sun plops into Sarasota Bay.

Yes, I'm talking about adjectives here. Each of us has an arsenal of them that we use and overuse while writing our books. You can find yours by clicking on a word in your Word document and doing a find (control F), and the navigation bar will show you the 142 uses of the word *amazing*.

Too much, too many. Too boring.

Using that little trick to locate the overused words (and you really didn't even know you had typed those words that much, did you?), take them one at a time, navigate through the manuscript, and substitute better, stronger, and different descriptors.

I know that a program called Grammarly can flag these overuses and suggest substitutions.

My point is this: be aware of words you overuse and take another pass just to spice them up a bit.

How to Find (Discover, Locate, Land on) the Right Word

I have been taking college courses on writing during my professional working years because I can. The University of Nebraska at Omaha allows those of us of a certain age free courses, and I took a class on essays as a stretch because I don't like writing short form.

Of course, the experience is eye-opening. One assignment was to interview someone and write a profile. I chose my favorite creative nonfiction writer, Marilyn Coffey, who, at eighty-something, has such wisdom and a gift for choosing the right word. I mean how many authors do you know who can use words such as *scoundrels* and *thieves* so effectively in a book title?

On writing, she offers this advice: "Don't give up." And when I pressed her about her apparent gift for finding just the right word, she said with surprise, "Oh! I research them."

On Google. No digging around in dictionaries or thesauruses.

"When I write, I don't pay attention to the language, really. I just let it go out as it will [and she demonstrates with a flutter of fingers], and then, as I rewrite, I get into these questions of should I use, 'The sky is blue,' or should I say something else?"

And on her Google search, how does she know when she finds the right word?

"It arrives." Said with a flourish like a pianist to punctuate the thought.

I can't top that advice.

And So Forth

Anybody who suffered through Latin class in high school has my sincerest sympathies. I was a French student, happily, with a fairly sound background that has absolutely no value to me now unless I go to France.

But the Latin gave you an advantage. If you paid attention, you may have retained some of the derivations and roots more than the rest of us. We use these Latinisms and don't even think about it, or know what they mean, etc.

Etcetera etcetera etcetera. And so forth. I figure new authors start down a sentence, list some items, keep writing, and then run out of steam and go with the easy etc. to mean whatever comes next in this list. It's lazy writing, of course. Let me help you smooth those sentences.

Avoid i.e. and e.g. as well. By using *such as* or *for example*, you are saying the following items are examples and not a complete list. No need for *etc.* Let me show you:

Not this:

"Identify four of five key categories that you want to base your reinvention strategy around (e.g., production, process, sales and marketing, delivery)."

Do this:

"Identify four of five key categories that you want to base your reinvention strategy around (for example, production, process, sales and marketing, and delivery)."

Not this:

"When writing this book, I had several Google alerts active using words such as *reinvention*, *pivot*, *thinking outside of the box*, *business recovery*, etc."

Do this:

"When writing this book, I had several Google alerts active using words such as *reinvention*, *pivot*, *thinking outside of the box*, and *business recovery*."

On Slanguage

To be honest with you—and because this isn't my first rodeo when it comes to plain talk about language (its use, misuse, and cliché)—I thought I'd lean in and discuss the state of our *slanguage* in a short essay that even linguist John McWhorter would enjoy, because as I tried to think outside the box (or sentence or paragraph, so to speak), I realized at the end of the day that we're, like, reaching out to define truth to power in this case, and if we're ever going to think inside the box, leaning in, and be able to land this plane, then we need to eschew obfuscation, gain traction, gather the troops around the watercooler, and understand that nobody in the C suite will ever give kudos regarding the top line of our thinking on this, no matter what our expertise or wheelhouse—whatever—therefore, to make a long story short (except in this, a one-sentence essay), let's dump the clichés that have crept into our speaking and writing, LOL, and use plain English [insert emoji here]. Full stop.

I don't think this point about avoiding clichéd language needs any further discussion.

Passive Sentences: The Grammar Book, the Boy, and the Ball

Remember the dreaded red-and-white grammar book in high school? The tiresome explanation of active and passive sentences? *The ball was thrown by the boy.* Why the hell didn't the boy just throw the damn ball? Those examples helped us sort out active from passive sentences (and we never understood why we had to in the first place).

There are other errors you could be making in your writing. It is a problem when you use weak and pathetic passive sentence construction, and as I point these out, you should have an aha moment. They lurk in your writing. As the first two sentences in this paragraph do. You see, I started those sentences with *there are* and *it is.*

I know you were snoozing in English class when Miss Barker (well, she was my beloved English teacher at Central High School in Sioux City, Iowa, and I adored her) explained about the passive sentence structure. I didn't know it at the time, but these sentences would help me make a decent living just by correcting them for unsuspecting writers.

Let's take a look at the offending sentences. Here is the do-this, not-that list:

Not this:

There are other errors you could be making in your writing.

Do this:

You could be making plenty of other errors in your writing.

Not this:

It is a problem when you use weak and pathetic passive sentence construction, and as I point these out, you should have an aha moment.

Do this:

When you use weak and pathetic passive sentences, you make your readers die a thousand deaths. Boring. Boring. Boring. When I pointed these out, did you have an aha moment?

Miss Barker may have cringed about the one-word sentences with no subject or verb, but too bad. Language changes. Conventions change. Which is why I won't go into that ridiculous discussion of whether to split an infinitive or whether to not split is okay. It's okay.

Or start a sentence with a conjunction, like this sentence. I love the sentences that start with *and*. Or end a sentence with a preposition. Fine. Whatever.

How do you know if your writing is effective? Simple. Readers understand what you have written. It's that simple.

Just Plain Wordy Sentences

Consider this sentence: "From the thousands of people I've worked with over the years, I've come to the conclusion that there are six major obstacles that you are likely to face throughout your reinvention journey and in life for that matter." (from Nils Vesk's *Reinvention Sprint*)

Okay. Makes sense. But it's wordy.

At North Junior High School, we used to diagram sentences, which tells you a lot about my age. The practice was a helpful way to sort out the subject and verb in a sentence. Then all the other clauses and adverbs were stuck onto the diagram (a map, really, of a sentence). The exercise helped us eighth graders pick out the subject and verb, the essence of the sentence.

Of course, that was the year I did my book report on *Catcher in the Rye*, and the teacher whose name I have long forgotten, went batshit crazy. But I digress except for this first sentence of sixteen-year-old Holden Caulfield's story:

"If you really want to hear about it, the first thing you'll probably want to know is where I was born, and what my lousy childhood was like, and how my parents were occupied and all before they had me, and all that David Copperfield kind of crap, but I don't feel like going into it, if you want to know the truth."

I won't make you poke your eyes out trying to find the subject and verb here in this masterful work of J. D. Salinger.

Happily, no editor tinkered with Salinger's opening salvo of his controversial book that nearly got me kicked out of English class and my mother called, "Did you know your daughter was reading this book?"

Let's go back to the opening sentence and my more succinct revision:

"From the thousands of people I've worked with over the years, I've concluded that you are likely to face six major obstacles throughout your reinvention journey and in life for that matter."

Examine your bloated sentences for ways to shorten and get to the heart of the message. I find that people who dictate/write their books tend to create these long and often convoluted sentences. Fine. Get the words down, and then get out your pruning shears.

Unclear Antecedents and Other Ways to Make Your Readers Want to Bludgeon You to Death

When you write, you know what you are saying. Memoir writers have the toughest time with writing scenes. Why? Because you were there. You can see the action. You see the scene from your childhood and write: "I remember the day my sister fell out of the tree swing and ran home crying. She wouldn't stop crying. I found out later she had broken her arm. *It* was a childhood memory, and I'll never forget *it*." But your readers don't see *it* unless you describe *it*.

Let me take another run at that last scene and fill in where the **unclear antecedents** (*it*) are used because your readers don't see this scene: "My seven-year-old sister and I climbed the massive maple tree in Margy's shady backyard next to the creek that meandered through the neighborhood. As the older sister, by two years, I let her grab the worn car tire hanging from a frayed rope so she could be first to try the swooping drop.

"As she grabbed onto the rope, not quite seated inside the tire, I let go, and she plummeted to the ground and landed on her right arm. She started crying immediately and ran home, cradling her arm, glancing back to give me that dirty look only sisters shared. Later, she was taken to the ER and came home with a huge white plaster cast. I was sorry I let go too soon, but I wouldn't tell her that."

Watch for overuse of *it* because when you go back to your work, you can find plenty of places where description can just spill out on the page, as you search your memory for those scenes. Imagine you are writing a screenplay. Especially in memoir, you are reliving past times. Get the description out. Use all your senses. Ask yourself, what did the kitchen in my childhood home look like? What smells bring back those memories? Do you see the rotary phone on the wall? Can you still see your mother sitting at the gray metal kitchen table? Can you still taste the grilled cheese sandwiches?

Business book writing can't call on such vivid memories as memoir can, but you can still pay attention to unclear antecedents. Here's an example where I prompted author Gary Huff in his leadership book, *So, Dad, How Do You Get to Be a CEO?*, to give more detail:

"Real integrity is living your values no matter what the outcomes. Your integrity and reputation are all that you have. Guard *it* and protect *it* with all of your efforts and truly live *it* with your actions, not just with words."

In a marginal comment, I asked the author to explain the unclear antecedents. Here is the final edited version:

"Real integrity is living your values no matter what the

outcomes. Your integrity and reputation are all that you have. Guard your integrity and truly live your values with your actions, not just with words."

Detail can also come with **dialogue**. Consider dialogue your friend. Of course, you don't have a recording of the actual he said/she said, but it's fair game to reconstruct dialogue to the best of your memory without embellishment (embellishment would take your work into the realm of fiction).

I often use this example in my writing classes. Brian Bogdanoff was a homicide detective when he wrote the true crime story of his solving a deadly case involving gangs and drugs. From the scene where he finally arrested the bad guys, here is what his original manuscript said:

ORIGINAL

As I spoke with each of them separately, I could see nobody wanted to talk yet, so I made it very clear to Preston and Gaylan that I was a homicide detective, not a narcotics officer, and this case that brought me to them was just getting started.

I asked him to use his senses to describe the scene, as if writing it as a movie. I pulled detail from him. He could see it. And now we had details down on paper for his readers to relive the interrogation scene too. See how much stronger and more vivid this description is?

REVISION

Gaylan was first. If someone was going to talk, I thought it would be Gaylan.

I walked into a fourth-floor interview room of the Criminal Investigation Bureau at downtown police headquarters. Gaylan was sitting at the same table where he'd been sitting for nine hours while we were searching his house, the recording studio, the lawn service, the remaining storage units, and his secondary houses.

His head was down, he looked up at me and said, "What's up, man?"

He's a big guy, twenty-four years old, and tired from sitting in a ten-by-ten room all day. He wasn't handcuffed, but there was a guard outside the door.

"You got big problems," I opened the conversation. "I got a receipt and inventory of all the stuff we recovered today, and it doesn't look good." I handed him a list of the property seized.

"I'm a homicide cop, and that's what this is all about, so you might be in your best position right now to tell me what you know," I said. "If someone else wants to talk first, they'll get all the good things that come with it." And he chose not to talk.

I gave the same spiel to Preston. He had the same attitude. He wasn't talking.

Roscoe and I then walked Gaylan to the jail elevator and rode it to the basement of the police station. We put our guns in the gun locker and walked him into jail. He's booked in for his marijuana charges and taken to his concrete ten foot by ten foot cell in solitary confinement, which on the street has earned the name "Bedrock."

We did the same procedure for Preston.

Used with permission from Brian Bogdanoff, author of *Three Bodies Burning: The Anatomy of an Investigation into Murder, Money, and Mexican Marijuana.*

And and Other Conjunctions You Were Told Never to Start a Sentence With

Miss Barker would have taken her red pen to sentences that started with conjunctions such as *and*, *but*, *or*, and *nor*. Today, those constructions have crept into our written word, and if they aren't overused or misused or abused, they are *not incorrect* (that double negative is to make a point that double negatives are not horrible creatures either).

And about those prepositions you are not to end a sentence *with*? The alternative can be awkward unless you rewrite the sentence more elegantly. Same with sentence fragments.

These are some of the no-nos we were drilled about in the *Harbrace College Handbook*. Which no one follows.

Your editor is not the grammar police, but a helpful editor will work with you to vary your sentence structures and reword when something can be said with more clarity.

Your First Colon-oscopy: Punctuation, Exclamation Marks, and Ellipses

If you don't know how to use the lowly and often forgotten semicolon, don't try. This book is not a usage lesson, and I won't bore you with the geeky stuff we editors love to discuss in the endlessly fascinating world of punctuation.

My favorite punctuation mark, however, is the **em dash**. Miss Barker never talked about the em dash. The em dash is longer than its cousin the hyphen. In fact, it's the length of the letter M—see? Use it after thoughts in a sentence—something like this. Make it by pressing the control + alt + minus (the minus key that's usually above the 9 in your keypad). No spaces on either side.

You'll see me using the em dash in this book because I love it. I edited a book by a Pulitzer Prize nominee, a journalist, who used the em dash in just about every sentence. I toned them down in his book.

The colon can also be your friend. Use the colon to introduce a list that is introduced by a complete sentence. Otherwise, introduce the list with no punctuation. First-time authors like to drop that colon in with every list.

In editing I see a few instances of comma misuse, so I'll mention them for you. When you have an introductory clause with a subject and a verb like this one, you put a comma after that introductory clause.

If the introductory words are *so* or *yet* or *now*, some writers put a comma, but it's not necessary. So I'll leave it up to you to decide. I opt for no commas unless there's a serious pause for meaning.

About those two independent clauses separated by a conjunction, here's an example: The author used two independent clauses, and she separated them with a comma.

These are two complete sentences with a subject and a verb each. Use the comma before *and*, *but*, *or*, and those conjunctions. This is a nonnegotiable comma. I see it missing a lot.

The negotiable comma is the serial comma that appears in a list before a conjunction: red, white[,] and blue. Is that comma before *and* necessary? Probably not in this sentence. But *Chicago* style says use the serial comma (sometimes called the Oxford comma), so we do, consistently, throughout a manuscript. If you don't put them in, consistently, tell your editor you don't want the commas inserted unless absolutely necessary for meaning.

If you're my author, I will allow you maybe five exclamation marks in an entire book. Otherwise, they're coming out.

I am reminded of why I have this aversion to exclamation marks. Three young women wrote a book titled *It's Really 10 Months: Delivering the Truth about the Glow of Pregnancy and Other Blatant Lies* in which they reprinted their emails to each other while they were pregnant at the same time. I removed thousands of exclamation marks during the edit. As if pregnancy wasn't its own emphatic time of life. So Natalie, Kim, and Celeste spoiled that exclamation mark for you and scarred me for life.

And that's all I have to say about punctuation. Period.

He, She, It, or Shit?

Before the world finally accepted the singular *they* (I'll explain in a second), we struggled with pronouns *he* and *she* and authors would use he or she alternately or he/she or leave a note at the beginning of a book, "I am using the pronoun he, but I mean that to be inclusive of she," and other nonsensical apologies for gender. Other authors would just write in the plural *they*.

None were elegant solutions to an odd quirk in American English.

But *Chicago* style finally anointed the singular *they* in 2017 with these words that are gold to an editor's ears:

Most often in English the pronoun *they* refers to a plural antecedent, but *they* can also be used to refer to a singular antecedent.

Instead of—

"For starters, why should an immature teenager, with no life experience, know what *he or she* wants to do for the forty-odd years of his or her working life?"

You can now say—

"For starters, why should an immature teenager, with no life experience, know what *they* want to do for the forty-odd years of *their* working life?" (from Robert Richey's book, *From Here to Retirement Wealth*)

—and feel comfortably correct. Still, I liked my solution combining she (s) and he (h) and (it) = shit. It didn't catch on.

Readability: Can You Understand Me Now?

You may recall hearing about Flesch scores, and although it sounds like some disgusting flesh-eating bacteria, the result was actually similar—creepy. Manuscripts were scoured by grammar and writing police for big words, words with many syllables, long sentences. The thinking was that short words and short sentences made the material understandable. Grade levels were assigned. So a fourth-grade reading level was considered a target.

Now think about that. Readability scores played into mistaken thinking about people's levels of intelligence. I haven't run a readability score for years, and I never bought into the theory.

Here is my theory: if you write something (a newspaper story, a magazine article, a book, a blog), and your target audience understands what you wrote, then your work is readable. Simple. Can you test your work out on a likely reader? Of course. If you have some beta readers or friends who fall into your target reader category (in other words, if you are writing history, and they are history readers, they fit), ask them to read an early draft of your work. Ask them questions to see if they understood your arguments or followed your logic. It might cost you a cup of coffee at Starbucks, but such advice is worth a latte.

One final point: ~~eschew~~ avoid those big words anyway. I have seen authors who use a thesaurus to turn simple words into pedantic expressions of their own need to sound, well, smart. They don't.

You Offend Me: The Sensitivity Read

In an era of #MeToo, Black Lives Matter, and just plain renewed awareness and sensitivity to our fellow human beings, an entire editorial movement has arisen to help authors avoid offending any reader.

Even our goddesses at the *Chicago Manual of Style* offices have changed their minds about the terms *Black* and *White* in reference to race. We now capitalize them.

But aside from the obvious controversy about capitalization, the issue is not so black and white anymore. Terms you may have used your entire life are now deemed insensitive (finally), and we editors and you authors can and must be aware of their use (and make changes).

I have long been editing him/her, he/she, but that's not what sensitivity really means. Bosses aren't always men. Nurses aren't always women. Flight attendants haven't been called stewardesses for a very long time, and you'd never use racial slurs.

Fortunately, the singular *they* has helped neutralize gender pronouns in narrative when people are pronoun sensitive. But conscious language and sensitivity reading goes far beyond gender pronouns.

Consider *mankind* and *middleman*. Why not *humanity* and *intermediary* or *go-between*? Instead of *layman*, use *layperson*. *Freshmen* are *first-year students*. A *foreman* is a *supervisor*, and a *chairman* can be a *chair* or *chairperson*.

Please recognize that you may be using words and phrasing you are not even aware of as being insensitive. This is the area known as conscious language.

Even as I drafted this section, I sought the guidance of Crystal Shelley, an editor far smarter than I am, to help explain this particularly thorny issue:

She said, "**Sensitivity reading** is a service that critiques how language and materials are presented when a writer is writing about identities or experiences they don't have. They'll hire a sensitivity reader who does have those identities or experiences to evaluate the accuracy of the writing in those areas.

"**Conscious language**, on the other hand, is more general and can—and should—be flagged by any editor. Examples include language that can be considered disrespectful, excluding, stigmatizing, or presumptive. For example, if a writer writes about business practices in China but they don't have direct experience, they may hire a sensitivity reader with direct experience to read the draft and assess how the topic has been handled. This would be different from an editor who flags all general conscious language issues they come across in the draft."

How might that look in a manuscript? Business book writers, for instance, often use workplace examples. They make up stories and names, and those names are usually Susan, John, Barbara, and Bob. Really? How inclusive will readers named Juan and Juanita and Dayshon and Imani and Jade and Kayvon feel? I encourage writers to consider the readership and the diversity of the workplace to be broader rather than narrower.

If terms such as *cisgender* and *Latinx* are unfamiliar to you, spend some time reading up about diversity and inclusion in these areas (and of course all these examples have exceptions and preferred usages):

- Gender (if the gender-neutral singular *they* doesn't fit, ask the person how they would like to be referred to)
- Race and racial slurs (ask if race matters in your book and if such a description is even relevant; racial slurs have no place in writing, and be sensitive in writing actual dialogue or attempts at jargon; Kansas recalled license plates with the sequential letter combination NGA because of insensitivity, and you think they would have learned because two years before the state recalled plates with JAP; question whether you use *Gypsy* and *gyp*, or *Jew*, *First Nation*, or *illegal alien* because you will be offending some readers)

- Appearance (fat shaming is real, *people living with obesity* is a move in the right direction)
- Age (*seniors* and *elderly* can be, instead, *older people*)
- Ethnicity (*Latinx* is a gender-neutral term within the gendered Spanish language but not widely accepted by the community)
- Disability (people are not *wheelchair-bound*, they *use a wheelchair*; someone doesn't *suffer from manic depression*, someone has bipolar disorder; *handicapped parking* is *accessible parking*; people are not crazy or nuts, they may have *mental health challenges* or be someone with a mental health history)
- Language (if you use foreign terms and customs, make sure you check them with a native speaker of that language; the story is that the Lakota braves in *Dancing with Wolves* were mistakenly speaking the feminine form)

We should celebrate every imaginable difference. My go-to sources are these:

- Conscious Style Guide (www.consciousstyleguide. com), a watchdog website where ever-changing language conventions are reported.
- Also San Francisco State University's Diversity Style Guide is www.diversitystyleguide.com).
- Here is an A to Z look at terminology: https://www. pacificu.edu/life-pacific/support-safety/office-equity-diversity-inclusion/glossary-terms.

- The Editorial Freelancers Association has a comprehensive Word List of Diversity and Contested Terms (need membership access).

In summary, I have added these writing tips to the Checklist at the back of this book. Make sure you comb your manuscript for these instances of overused words, meaningless words, punctuation no-nos, unclear antecedents, and conscious choices about people descriptions so you can fix them before your edit.

Chapter 10

Beta Readers: Who They Are and How They Can Help You Make Your Book Better

Sheryl Ness, a nurse from the Mayo Clinic in Minnesota, went to Italy and fell in love with the chef in a charming village restaurant. A real love story. A delicious love story because her memoir included the stories behind the many recipes of her new husband (yes, they married), especially his chocolate love cake that sparked this storybook romance.

But as she finished writing her draft, she was concerned. Like many first-time authors, she wondered if her story was good enough. She wanted to know if she had just the right amount of story balanced with recipes. Substantively, she worried she had included too much about the old boyfriend and whether she should integrate the recipe pages with the narrative or gather them at the back.

Sheryl and I agreed that these were questions a group of target readers (presumably also book buyers) would answer for her, so we conducted a beta read. I reviewed my contact list for likely female friends and other authors who loved to cook, loved fine dining, maybe traveled to Italy, and might be memoir readers. She also gave me some names of potential objective readers who were not her close friends but were friends of friends.

You see, anybody related to her by marriage, DNA, Facebook, or work were not going to be detached enough from her and her story. They knew her. And the thinking is that your mother-in-law, for example, may not be tough enough. Your spouse is going to tell you what you want to hear. So they're out.

We constructed a list of about ten questions that could not be answered by yes or no. We wanted real feedback and answers to the questions about content and placement of recipes so Sheryl could make more revisions to move her manuscript to final, with the kind input of readers. We sent them all the Word document by email and gave them the questions and two weeks.

With a nudge or two by email, we heard back from most. We looked for a pattern in the answers. One reader said she wanted to throw the author under a bus. The story was too sappy for her. Others raved and gushed about their love of Italy and Sheryl's adventures and story. The consensus was that the recipes were to be integrated with the story; there was too much about the old boyfriend so his story was out; and they wanted more description about the people in the tiny Tuscan village where Vincenzo owned the restaurant.

Sheryl was delighted. The final book is lovely (*Love in*

a Tuscan Kitchen). The recipes are to die for (and I can't live without my tiramisu), and that's how a beta read produces a truly sweet ending.

Sheryl's book benefited from the opinions of test readers, like a focus group, not just one person (an editor) who may or may not even be in that target reader group.

When an author is saying to me, "I'm just not sure I have the content right." "Do you think I put too much attention on this and not enough on that?" "Have I addressed all the concerns my readers will have about this model?"

That's when I pull out the beta reader suggestion.

You can find beta readers on Goodreads (a beta reader group) or among your writing critique group (but I'd put less weight on comments from the science fiction writer in the group if you're not writing science fiction). Or try a Facebook post to find friends of friends.

Should you pay beta readers? Most of the time, no. Avid readers love to be in on a new book. They unselfishly give of their time. I have had a writer give $20 Starbucks gift cards to readers who followed through and provided input (not everyone who agrees to read your draft will do so but more will respond if you dangle a carrot). You can also promise to put their name in the Acknowledgments section and send them a copy of the final book.

I have seen some so-called publishing services companies offering a beta read. These "reads" aren't a target market read. They use professional editors and writers to render an opinion, and sadly the results of the "read" are used to sell you their editing services. Beware.

Don't confuse a beta read with an editorial evaluation or editorial assessment, which I explain in detail in chapter 5.

The best beta reader process works well when readers respond to me instead of to the author directly. Then I can collate the responses, look for patterns of responses, interpret the advice from the readers, and insulate the respondents from the author so they can feel comfortable being candid.

With Sheryl's readers, the one who said, "I wanted to throw the author under a bus," provided perhaps the most valuable comments for the author. We knew they were authentic and took guts to say. Just because one reader goes off on the author and really does throw them under a bus, temper those comments with caution. That's one person's opinion. Even if that person is a book reviewer for the *New York Times Book Review*, it's still one person's opinion.

Never make major changes based on one person's comments. If a few beta readers mention that the discussion of the scenarios in chapter 6 need examples and your lame poetry you inserted as chapter openers was distracting, then consider this wise advice. Your market is giving you the best focus group reaction you could ever need. And that's when you discover the answer to this question: "Is this book any good?"

Writing a book requires a village. The next part of this book discusses the village people you need to get to publication and beyond the edit.

After the Edit: Now What?

Part III

Chapter 11

How to Work with Other Members of Your Book Production Team

Your editor is only one part of the production team when you write and publish a book. I am an editor, not an illustrator, cover designer, interior designer, or audiobook narrator and producer, or printer/publisher.

I have opinions, just like any book buyer and book reader and author, about cover design. I know if a book is difficult to read because the design of the pages is odd. I see crazy spacing in ebooks. So, again, I implore you not to do this process yourself.

Find members of your book production team just as diligently as you discovered your editor (and I refer you back to chapter 3). I tapped into the wisdom of my team, and here are some bullet points for you to consider.

Cover Designer

My advice is to work closely with your book designer on both your cover and interior. Both are designed elements of your book. Here are some truths and tips (and purely my opinion and a few from one of the most talented cover designers I've worked with, Domini Dragoone):

- Choose a cover designer who designs book covers. The graphic arts student son of your bridge partner or your cousin's friend who creates posters is not a book cover designer. Ask to see their portfolio to make sure they have experience in your genre (someone who designs dystopian covers and has never done a business book if you're writing a business book is not your best choice).
- Don't design your cover yourself. You can play art director with your cover designer, but don't overdirect. Let the designer come up with some initial concepts and go from there. Designers would prefer not to work with an image you like (a photographer friend who photographs wildlife, for example) or a photo of you, even if taken professionally, to create your cover. These types of images usually never work well in nonfiction, but you can talk with the designer and defer to their opinion on any images you provide. Sometimes a cool vintage family snapshot can work for memoir.
- When giving feedback to your cover designer, tell the designer what is working (size of the titling, colors, image, for example) as well as what you think is not working (for example, the font or the placement of the author's name). The designer needs to know what's working and leave it alone and build on that. Ask

the designer how they think a problem can be solved (let's say you aren't in love with your look of the title yet). Instead of saying, "Make it white," or "Make it bigger," ask the designer what they suggest next.

- Don't shoot a cover photo of yourself and ask your designer to design around your studio shot unless you want your designer to wince. If you are going to be the featured design on your cover, design the cover first and then shoot a photo to fit. Pre-shot photos rarely work out well.

- But do have a professional photo taken for your bio photo. You can use this head shot on the back cover with a short bio and on the About the Author page, and on your book's website as well as Amazon's Author Central page. It will be printed in black and white inside the book (tell the photographer you need a shot that looks amazing in color and in black and white). If your hair is black, don't shoot against a black background (photography 101).

- Look at similar and competing books in your genre. Create a gallery of covers and look for patterns. True crime books, for example, are often dark, even black. Health books tend to be white. Business books are using big blocky one-word titles right now. Trends change. Your goal is to look similar (don't be the book that looks different, because readers expect books to be similar looking), but be the best designed and most catchy title that says what the book is about. Be that book.

- If your cover is mostly white, make sure the designer puts a line around the cover for your images you post on Amazon and elsewhere. Otherwise your pretty white cover will float and be lost on a white background.

- Make sure your cover looks fantastic and that the titling is readable when your book cover is as small as your thumb (on your Amazon description page).
- If you want to buy a pre-made cover, good luck making that work, but it's not impossible and certainly cheaper.
- If you want to design your own cover, you will be among the authors whose covers look homemade, and I will use your covers as examples of what not to do in my classes.
- Covers cost anywhere from hundreds, to even a thousand or more. Judge the designer by their experience and references. Like the adage about tattoos, "Good tattoos aren't cheap, and cheap tattoos aren't good." Do you think someone with enough experience will charge just $50 for a cover? Don't be their learning curve.
- Cover design is not something you can or should do on Canva or your iPhone app.
- If one designer just can't give you what you want, stop tinkering. Find another designer with a different eye.
- Freelancer sites showcase designers' portfolios. But if you love a particular book's cover and it seems to work in your genre, check the Read Inside feature on Amazon and see if the designer is credited on the copyright page and track that person down. Most cover designers have websites.
- Should you put your three cover concepts on Facebook and ask your so-called friends to vote?

Here's the problem with polling. You won't get a consensus because people "like" different things. Think of your cover as a tool to communicate what the book is about. The question to ask, then, is not, Which book cover do you like? but this: Does this cover communicate what my book is about? The better group to ask are people who fit into your target reader category. I also like to run covers by bookstore owners and booksellers and librarians. They often have a real eye for what readers think.

Illustrator

- If your book has charts, tables, graphs, illustrations, cartoons, or other types of hand-drawn or computer-generated art, you'll want to identify an illustrator and direct them in the various images you need. Sometimes the images include words, and this is where editing and illustration need to talk to each other.

- Sometimes your interior designer can also be your illustrator and can certainly build tables and charts and graphs so typefaces match the book interior typefaces.

- Don't plunge ahead and hire an illustrator and create your images with captions and wording only to find out later you are misspelling words or not hyphenating properly. Have your editor edit/see/approve the wording you give to your illustrator first. Otherwise, you may find yourself going back for revisions to your illustrations, and that could get costly.

- Make sure you own the illustrations and that the

illustrator is doing this as work for hire. Have a written agreement or email. Illustrations should be unique to you with images that are either in the public domain or licensed.

- I know people have good luck on some of the freelancer sites such as Fiverr and 99Designs and Reedsy.
- While you're at it, have your illustrator create a logo for your publishing company (to be used on your book spine, back cover, title page, and all the T-shirts and mugs you're going to make for your friends).
- Try not to get involved in any legal hassles over images. I consult Helen Sedwick (www. HelenSedwick.com), lawyer and author of guides on legal issues for self-publishers.

Photographer and Photographs

- Keep Helen Sedwick's book handy if you are using photos. Life can get tricky when it comes to finding the owner of a photo and depicting popular images, brand names, and trade names.
- Every photo needs a caption. Identify who and what are in the photos: who (from left), where, when taken, what's happening. No exceptions, even your author photo needs your name under it.
- If you didn't take the photo yourself, you need permission to use the photo. Period. Richard Stanley paid the Getty archive for use of the prison cell photo from their collection in his *Up on Game* books. It was exactly the cell where he spent eight years. He had no other photos of it, and in his case a photo was worth

well over a thousand words, and he paid almost that much for its use. We also tracked down a photographer who did a photo shoot of his prison for a feature story, and the photographer gladly let him reprint several photos from his shoot that were not originally published with the story, for a reasonable fee.

- Rita Rae Roxx was an eighties rock groupie. She and her trusty little camera took hundreds of photos with rock stars backstage and "really" backstage, if you know what I mean. She owns those photos, so permission was not an issue. They added immeasurably to her memoir, *Once Upon a Rock Star*. Did she need permission to print her snapshots of famous people? The lawyers said no.

- You cannot find and use photos from the internet. Someone owns them, and you have to find that owner and get written permission. The owner may want you to pay a fee for the use. You can hire professional permissions services to do the research work for you. It all costs money but saves you legal fees on the other end.

- If a kind photographer allows you to use their photos or if you've paid a fee for use, ask them how they wish the credit line to read (example: Used with permission from Frank's Fine Fotos.). Print the credit line on the photos and/or on the copyright page.

- You cannot reprint an image from a newspaper. Contact the paper's archivist about their permission process and fees.

- If in doubt, don't use an image.

Interior Book Designer

- For your book's interior, ask the designer (could be the same person as your cover designer) to choose a readable font that is used in books for your text. Fonts with serifs work well for readability. Those are the little squiggly things on the letters. Headlines and cover titling can be in sans serif font (no squiggly things).

- Choose a book size that reflects most of the books in your genre. If most are 6 x 9 (a standard size), use that. If many are 8 ½ x 5 ½, then join the crowd. You can find the book size on the Amazon description page. If bookstores are still around, spend an afternoon with a vente latte and scour all the books in your genre for size, price, look, content, and competing features. Libraries are also ideal places to browse the competition (minus the coffee). Do the same research on Amazon description pages.

- For pricing, be guided by similar and competing books in your genre. Do some research, even a spreadsheet, with similar and competing books to get a sense of where your book fits. Don't be the highest priced soft cover and ebook, nor the lowest. Here are the categories to research from a book's description page on Amazon:
    * Size
    * Price for ebook and paperback
    * Number of pages (compare with the number of your finished pages)
    * Recency (unless a book is a classic in your field, just look at books published within the last three years)
    * Amazon rank (as long as you're doing the research,

take a look at the overall Amazon ranking)
  * Categories (under the Amazon ranking, note the
    categories competing books fall under, because
    that's where you want to be competing generally)
  * To find more competing books, view the sections
    titled Customers Also Viewed or Customers
    Also Bought
- Hardcover? Nah. You can't create a hardcover
  book on Amazon's KDP anyway. You need to use
  IngramSpark. When was the last time you bought
  a hardcover book and paid $30? Right. You're not a
  library. Libraries will carry your book in paperback.
  COVID changed a lot of reading habits and drove
  readers to ebooks and audiobooks.
- Your ebook designer may or may not be your interior
  designer. Ebooks require special coding so they scroll
  smoothly in all ebook formats without page numbering.
  This is more a mechanical process than a design
  process, but readability is the key. Find and work with
  an ebook coder who can show you examples first. You
  don't want to see clunky scrolling, awkward placements
  for graphics and photos, or big blank spaces.

Indexer

- First, decide if your book requires an index. Most
  nonfiction consumer books do not need an index. If
  you're writing about history and historical figures,
  then perhaps an index would be helpful to history
  buffs. Business/leadership books won't benefit from an
  index (there are always exceptions). Memoirs, no.

- When I edited the history of the Omaha Playhouse, the book publishing services company contracted with a professional indexer (yes, indexers are a specialty) because the book contained tons of names of some famous (Henry Fonda, for example) and local actors and extras, and one of the main selling points was to consult the index and see if a family member was included in the narrative or photos.
- Resist the simple solution to use software to create an index. The software is not AI and cannot judge whether the reference to the Civil War on page 14 is relevant for someone using an index. Indexes are constructed page by page as someone reads final page proofs (this is the very last step before publication) and records page numbering and subheadings (for example, battles of the Civil War under Civil War). Indexing is expensive.
- Not every key word or concept is important enough to be indexed. You need to think about how people will search inside your book, what they want to search for.
- If an author wants to create an index, I ask them to create a list of key words first and subheadings under those key areas. If they create their index themselves, they can use the list as a guide.
- You can find indexers where you find editors. Many are or were librarians. Makes sense.
- In lieu of an index, I ask authors to consider beefing up their Contents page. Here's why. If you list all your chapter titles and then all the subheadings at least at the top level, a reader can get a magnificent overview of the complete book. Because so many

books are purchased online, potential buyers can't look at the index anyway, but by using Amazon's Look Inside feature, they can view the table of contents online and see all its glorious subheadings. Use this as a marketing tool as well, as you put your book together. (Which is another reason those chapter titles and subheadings should be fascinating as hell and super descriptive.)

- I have chosen not to index this book because my Contents page is loaded with helpful navigation. And consider this: Nobody looks at an index in an ebook because page numbering is fluid in an ebook as readers shuffle the size of the text on their reading devices. No page numbers (think about it). Of course, page numbers in an audiobook would be foolish. Get with the technology, people, and dump those indexes except for that rare book that can benefit from having one.

Audiobook Production

- With more and more books being available as audiobooks, and more readers actually opting to hear their books, I foresee much more attention to how books sound in the months and years ahead.
- Oh, but you want to record your own book. Bad idea. In fact, horrible idea. Unless you are a professional voice, you'll have flubs and extraneous sounds, even page turning (read from a computer or iPad screen instead and use caution with mouse clicks), and all that is amateur hour. Pay the money for a pro.
- Books with photos and graphics can become

audiobooks. You upload a PDF file of the graphics, which your audio readers can download and see.

- In *Mozart in the Garden*, the author had tons of family photos with exceptionally long and fascinating captions, almost as part of the narrative. The audiobook "voice" and engineer, Benjamin McLean, masterfully narrated the captions as well, even for listeners who could not see the photos. Be creative if this is your book.

- Ben taught me that audiobooks need special preparation before the pro voice can do their best work. Go through your PDFs or ebook version (which is what the voice will read from so there is no sound of paper shuffling, a pro tip) and use marginal notes to show pronunciations. Don't assume the reader knows that your family name is pronounced WEN-del not wen-DELL until you tell them. I've heard about readers having to remaster after pronouncing a name incorrectly throughout an entire book. Place names, people names, and even big words can be phonetically flagged for your voice reader. Don't assume they know.

- A phone call with the voice to go over the tricky pronunciations is always a plus.

- Listen to every chapter and follow along with your copy of the PDFs. Forgive a miss here and there, but flag for correction any missed words, mispronunciations (especially critical with foreign names and places), or missed sections. If you are hoping for dialect, work with the voice ahead of time on samples.

- Sometimes your written words may sound awkward when you hear them. That's the not-so-subtle difference between the written word and spoken word. Your voice/reader may subtly adjust with contractions, for example, and that's perfectly fine.

- Check out www.ACX.com, which is Amazon's audiobook platform directly to Audible where listeners download audiobooks. You can audition a voice/narrator who will engineer your book and upload it to the platform. Eventually your ebook, paperback, and audiobook will link up on one Amazon description page.

- You pay per finished hour (prices vary widely based on experience of the voice person). ACX decides the pricing of your audiobook, sorry. If you go with ACX as your exclusive distributor, you get more money in royalties. Be mindful of the wait time for ACX to quality check and finally upload your audiobook to Amazon—could be weeks.

- And there's one final little gem: Even if you have had a proofreading and several rounds of edits, your audiobook reader might find and report back to you a few stray typos or missed words or extra words during the audio recording. It's like a final edit, in a sense.

Your Local Librarians

Librarians can be your new best friends. Like you, they love books. They love connecting readers with books readers want to read. Does your book cover and title give readers enough information about your book? Is it apparent your book is a memoir (you can add a small tag "A Memoir" on the cover)? If your book is a novel, you can add a tag too (A Novel).

The biggest pet peeve librarians have is not knowing immediately from the look, the title, and the back cover description what your book is about and where it should be shelved. People who read business books look in the nonfiction shelves (literally and online) for those books. A memoir miscategorized as a novel will languish on the wrong shelf.

Tip: You can place a line about genre on the book itself above the bar code on the back cover (BUSINESS/LEADERSHIP) for example, or place this line at the top of the back cover. Helps with shelving.

Shelby Janke, my favorite librarian at my local Waterloo, Nebraska, library, has given me some pointers:

- **First things first: use your local library.** Create a relationship with your librarians as a library user first, and as an author second. This will pay off when you are planning book events and need a place to bring readers together. Create a relationship with your librarians not only for the sake of promoting your book, but to create a sense of community with fellow book experts and recommenders. Library staff are more likely to host an event with an author they already know who appreciates the library and has a connection to its services.

  Librarians are trained to be expert researchers, material recommenders, and early readers. Some larger libraries have a librarian or department specifically dedicated to helping writers complete the best manuscript possible. Use them during your writing process and in your reading life.

- **Donate copies of your book.** Small libraries have small budgets with which to purchase new books. If you're a first-time author, chances are that book vendors for libraries do not have your new book in their inventory to purchase from. Thus, libraries may not have an opportunity to purchase your title from their usual book vendor.

  Here's where you come in: donate a couple of copies to your local library along with your contact information and a synopsis of the book. Sign the books if you feel so moved. Donating your new book to your library is a sure-fire way to add your book to the library's collection without jumping through purchasing hoops, allowing community members to find your book in the library catalog.

- **Set up an author event.** I'm not a big fan of sitting in a bookstore or library with your book on a table and hoping likely readers/buyers come by. But if you bill your event as a reading or talk, you are much more likely to have an audience.

  For example, if your memoir has a local setting, name your presentation "The Ghosts of Hummel Park," local author's memoir features spooky setting. Or how about "The 10 Traits for Success Every New Manager Needs to Know," local author and former CEO presents a talk at 7:00 p.m. at the Swanson Library. One more: "The Cold Case Murders Nobody Knew About (Until Now)," detective Ace Ventura reads from his new book and so on. As you know, author events and book readings are one way to promote your new book.

Many libraries have a minimal fee or no fee for hosting book-related events in their meeting space. Be sure to bring copies of your book for audience members to purchase the night of your event. Ask friends and family to come help fill up the room. Keep your event to an hour or less. Readers love to ask questions and solve problems, so it is best to keep your speech and book reading portion to thirty minutes or less and then allow another thirty minutes for a Q&A session. It is easier to set up an event at your local library if you already have an established relationship with them.

- Libraries like hard cover books, but they are not mandatory.

- **Book club suggestions:** Make your book available at discount pricing to buy directly from you if your local library buys, say, twenty copies and make yourself available to talk to clubs who read your book (in person or via Zoom). If your book has local interest, all the better. Readers like to make connections with authors. Be a rock star.

Shelby knows my favorite authors and suggests others in the same genre. So when a new C. J. Box or William Kent Krueger book comes out, she puts me at the top of the list, if I haven't contacted her first to reserve the book. If your memoir is another *Glass Castle*, your librarian BFFs can suggest your book to patrons who are browsing in the memoir aisle. Many libraries have shelves just for local authors. You want your book to be there too.

Do this: Go to your local library or libraries. Introduce yourself. A signed copy of your book and a dozen donuts help endear you and your book to library staff (put some business cards inside the box). Ask to speak to the acquisitions librarian (the one who buys books). Donate a copy of your book or three to the library. Give them a one-sheet of info about your book including ISBN numbers and invite them to buy/stock more copies of your book.

Your Local Independent Bookstore

Struggling because of the nature of book sales and distribution, your local independent bookstore is a survivor. Support them.

Go in and introduce yourself (with another dozen donuts). Ask if they'd consider stocking your book and buying directly from you at wholesale pricing (expect they will want at least a 40 to 55 percent discount off retail). I advise not giving them books on consignment. You want an outright sale.

Tell them you will mention that readers can buy the book locally when you're doing local media such as radio shows and will put the bookstore name on your book's website too ("available on Amazon and at the Bookworm and local libraries").

Again, explore the idea of your book being suggested for book clubs (many of whom buy in quantity from the local bookstore). Make discounts (and yourself) available to book clubs.

Be responsive when they need more books to sell. Generally, avoid a signing because the bookstore usually wants you to invite your friends to come in and buy, and you've already sold books to everybody you feel comfortable strong-arming. But if the bookstore has a local author event, be there with a smile, a stack of books, a Sharpie, a banner, and a plate of brownies.

Better yet, suggest the bookstore host a talk or reading based on your book, as I suggested you do with libraries.

When Amazon's KDP Is Your Publishing Platform

- Have fun navigating KDP. I have viewed many webinars about how to get through the screens on KDP to get your book uploaded there, about how to order your author copies through KDP at Amazon's low wholesale author pricing, and how to change your pricing and descriptions. Find one of these webinars or search on YouTube. Watching these is well worth the time to do it all right when it comes to best description, most likely keywords (you are allowed seven strings of phrasing), best categories (you are allowed two but can add more), pricing, date of release, ISBN assignment, your checking account where beaucoup bucks will be deposited every month, and more.

- Before you press the button on KDP to go live, order one copy of your paperback book with your low author price. When it is delivered to your door, make sure it looks good, is printed correctly, that all pages are present, gutters not too tight, cover colors pop, and then order your author copies in small batches of twenty to fifty at a time (my recommendation).

- Also claim your Author Central page (authorcentral. amazon.com or author.amazon.com) and enter your bio, book reviews, even author photos and blog there.

When Someone Else Is Your Publisher

- Be guided by your publishing company and their requirements, but, as author, you may not have much say in your cover design or interior. You may not be consulted about your titling or size or pricing.
- On the other hand, you won't have to navigate KDP if someone else is publishing your book under their publishing company name and ISBNs.
- You will have to (and want to) review your PDFs for error.
- Many authors hire their own editors (and I am honored to work with authors who have publishing contracts) because I'm on the side of the author and can advocate for them.
- One more caution: Many companies say they are publishers but are, in reality, companies that scam authors and make money on the authors, not on direct book sales except to the author at high prices. See my earlier discussion of how to find these types of arrangements and avoid them or go into the deal with your eyes wide open.

Chapter 12

The Chapter on Writing That I Didn't Want to Include (But Here It Is)

When I outlined this book, I told myself to do what I tell authors to do: stick to the knitting. Tell your story, write your book, don't stray from the subject, and any material that doesn't fit gets cut.

I'm violating my premise that this book is about editing. I am going to address writing, but I have convinced myself that no one would need an editor unless they write, so here we go.

What I Tell My Writing Classes about How to Write

For over a decade, I have had the honor to teach a non-credit class at Metropolitan Community College in Omaha called How to Write Your Book and later How to Write

Your Story. At least four times a year, students gather in a classroom to hear what I have to say about writing a book.

For someone like me who spends ten to twelve hours a day heads-down at a computer keyboard in front of a screen of scrolling words, facing a classroom of eager learners is incredibly fun. These are noncredit adult education students. In other words, generally older people who have a bucket list project and time.

Over the years many have gone on to write and publish their books. I have edited a few and advised on others. Such gratification, and I thank them for sharing their stories with me during these classes. COVID brought a halt to in-person classes. But COVID gave me the time to write this book, and perhaps I can reach more than a classroom of people with these words on paper without the PowerPoint.

After one three-hour Saturday session, I was distressed when some feedback came my way from one of the administrative coordinators. She said, "A student called and told us she still didn't know how to write a book after she attended your class. She said she didn't really get any information on how to do it."

Wait, what?

For three hours, I had used my best PowerPoint slides, notes, and examples. I showed books other students who had been in my class had written. I even showed typos and cartoons, demonstrated how to use Track Changes, and offered my best advice on how to stop staring at a blank page. I brought donuts.

What this student wanted was for me to tell her how to write her story. Can't be done. I'm not her. I don't know her story. Short of hiring a ghostwriter and someone to interview her and write her story for her, this student just didn't realize that she is the driver of her story. We editors are not mind readers (although I have often tried to tell my kids that I am). We can't pull something out of you. You have to do the work and get the words on paper.

It's that simple—and that difficult.

Oh, yes, I have tips for writing, and if you need them, finish this chapter.

(Not So) Silly Writing Tips to Get Words on Paper

Imagine the first writer's block. I recall clipping a cartoon showing a caveman with a rudimentary stick staring at a large, blank rock.

Today's equivalent of the blank rock may be a computer screen, and your process may seem like this:

For those of you listening via audiobook, the image shows the bulk of the time surfing the net and shopping online, checking eBay, or snacking (that bag of chips on your desk didn't just disappear). Or typing t-h-e and then deleting it. When in fact the actual time spent writing is a fraction of an hour.

When you sit down to write (and there's a problem right there; you may not do well sitting down), do you find yourself with a sudden urge to clean out a file drawer? Throw in a load of laundry? Search the internet for ways to clean wine stains out of carpet? Check the refrigerator for the third time? Bake a cake instead?

You have something to say, but what's holding you back? The answer may have more to do with the type of writer you are than about what you have to say.

In my writing classes, I ask my students to consider this question: When you go somewhere new, do you prefer to tap the address into a smartphone GPS and **hear** the turn-by-turn directions? Or do you stop and ask directions? Or do you just want to **see** the map? Maybe you wing it and get lost before you stop and ask directions. Which technique do you use?

If you want to hear the directions, you are an audio learner. If you want to see the map, consider yourself a visual learner. And those who wing it would be considered kinesthetic learners.

Let's translate that into writing techniques.

The I-Need-to-Hear-It Writer

The audio learner may well be an audio writer. You are easily distracted by sound. So the birds chirping outside take your attention away from the computer. The furnace clicking on and off, the clock ticking, the refrigerator cycling, a hum from somewhere—all distract your brain from the task at hand.

Audio writers are fascinated with sound, and we can harness that ability to help in the writing process because audio people are often magnificent storytellers. Capture those thoughts in words by dictating a story, a scene, a paragraph, a description of a crowded train station.

I recommend the Voice Memos on your iPhone and various speech-to-text apps like Speechy (free) and Dragon (paid) that turn your sounds into words. You then email those dictated files to your computer and have raw words on paper, so to speak, without keyboarding.

Another app called Rev captures sound/dictation and conversation even among two or more people. You send off the files to Rev transcribers and have written text within hours (for a fee based on per-minute recording). I've worked on memoirs written, rather dictated, entirely on Rev. I use Rev to capture interviews and oral histories too.

Your version of Word may already have speech-recognition software built in. You just need an external microphone (or headset) and talk to yourself. Use Word's Help feature and search *text-to-speech* for directions on finding this well-hidden bonus you may have right in front of you.

Desperate to just capture a thought and you either have no paper or pen or hands free to write? Phone yourself and leave yourself a voice message.

Another option is to tell your story to someone else, in an interview format. Use a recorder. Have the interview transcribed and start with that as raw background.

The I-Need-to-See-It Writer

The visual learner needs to see the big picture. These writers make outlines (outlines can turn into the book's table of contents). They use index cards for ideas and shuffle them or lay them out on a table to visually see the story as it unfolds. Post-It Notes do the same thing when placed on a board or table, as a storyboard. Others may simply draw out the plotline through time for each character.

A storyboard with notes can help you lay out your book. Even J. K. Rowling used a notebook paper page with timelines in blocks and character development plotted out linearly to write *Harry Potter*.

A storyboard helps you visualize your book.

Do you identify with this type of writer? I don't know about picture and a thousand words, but doodles and drawings can sometimes make the unclear clear, like when I was buying special nails for affixing new siding, and the associate was saying, "Blah blah blah," (that's what I heard until I asked him to draw a picture). Do you ever find yourself telling someone to "draw me a picture" or drawing one yourself?

The act of drawing will help you organize and "see" the story. A mind map, therefore, is you drawing a picture of your plot, your characters, your complete story, a chapter, a through line, a story arc. Your central theme is usually the center point, and the subplots or characters branch out from that main theme. Let me draw you a picture.

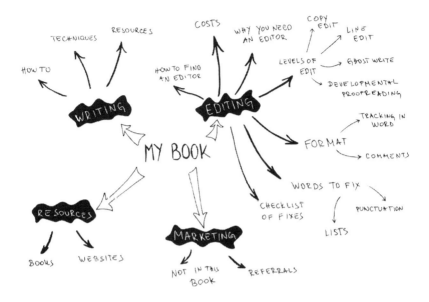

A mind map can help you visualize the entire
book like my mind map for this book.

Oh, it's like an outline. Yes, and even a tried-and-true outline is an ideal way to lay out your book (especially in nonfiction). Outlines don't need to be elaborate or detailed, and you don't need software, just a page of notebook paper. Mind maps can help you visual writers get started.

The Quirky Kinesthetic Writer

Neither visual or audio driven, the kinesthetic writer needs movement, which is why sitting down at a computer/laptop isn't going to work well.

So stand up. Put your laptop on the kitchen counter. Or take a walk and then come back and dump your brain onto paper.

We know the best ideas come when we are least expecting them. Thus the brain is tricked, during activity, to trigger a bright idea. Do you know the three most common scenarios for ideas to jump into your head (P.S.: Those ideas are already there.)? The answer is while sleeping, driving, or taking a bath/shower.

What is it about water? If you're stuck for an idea, wash the dishes. Put your hands in water. Or take a bath. I go kayaking.

If those ideas pop into your head while driving, be sure to grab your dictation device and capture it. Or for safety's sake, pull over and write it down.

Use sleeping as a trigger to set your intention before you go to bed. Keep a paper and pen or smartphone dictation device handy so you can brain dump it the moment you awaken.

One of my kinesthetic authors would take long runs and return to his computer with a jumble of ideas and thoughts and brain dump immediately into his computer. Sometimes he'd type, but as his thoughts came too quickly for his fingers, he'd dictate on voice recognition software.

Some writers need to change their venues. That's why we hear about prolific novelists such as William Kent Krueger thanking the staff in the coffee shops where he writes for allowing him to commandeer "booth #4" for far too long. Or Malcolm Gladwell who seeks out coffee shops when he travels, less for the brew and more for the right kind of distracting atmosphere. I have an app called Cofitivity that plays background noise: morning murmur or lunchtime lounge, for example. Personally, I find the noise annoying, but I'm a visual writer.

For some of us, our blank pages can be electronic or something else. Yes, some authors continue to write their books on yellow legal pads. One woman in my class confessed to typing on an old manual Remington Rand. We found her a transcriptionist who typed her writing into a Word document.

Start at the Beginning—or Not

When you are wondering where to start, just jump in. Anywhere. Somewhere. And not necessarily at the beginning. Write what feels right at the moment without the pressure to start at the beginning.

People writing memoirs like to start at the beginning chronologically, and that's fine to start with. But a smart editor can often see the big picture and move something life-defining to the opening chapter as a grabber for readers.

I worked with bank robber Richard Stanley who grew up in a gang-controlled San Diego neighborhood. The influences of his surroundings were tough to break out of. In fact, he started robbing banks and ended up in prison for nearly eight years.

He started his story at the beginning when he was doing petty shoplifting and stealing CDs from Target and reselling them to his classmates in school, in the fourth grade.

I revised the narrative to start with the defining moment in his life: his first adrenaline-powered, hands-sweating bank robbery. A stolen getaway car, hasty disguise, a quickly scratched note, "Put the money on the counter," and the need for cash to buy a meal at Taco Bell. In the following chapters, we dipped back as his story unfolded to pick up the backstory of his tumultuous childhood.

Or a narcotics sergeant who detailed his life on the street. In his initial working draft, Mark Langan started his memoir when he entered the police academy. In his final chapter, he told about how he shot and killed a drug dealer during an armed confrontation. What! That's our opener. The officer-involved shooting was his career-defining moment. Everything he did in his career in vice and narcotics and undercover led up to this shooting.

Of course, we moved the shooting to the front and let that story unfold as he dipped back in time to pick up the police academy, busting prostitutes, doing undercover work in gambling, and making no-knock drug busts. The story had a fascinating twist that wrapped up the drug dealer story nicely, and that became the last chapter. (If you're interested in true crime, this is Mark Langan's award-winning book *Busting Bad Guys*.)

But the lesson here is that both Stanley and Langan started at the beginning because that was comfortable to him and left it up to the editor to help reorganize. Editors can truly deliver stunning structure when you have it all there in the first place.

Think you have no time to write? Make time or schedule the time. Get up early and grab some time before work or school. Say no to outside activities. Start with just five minutes a day. Then increase it to ten minutes. Build the habit of confronting the blank page.

What about Writing Software and Tools?

I'm often given manuscripts that were created in Scrivener, which is an app or program that helps you organize your writing. Disclaimer: I have never used it. Here's why. I sat in on a webinar demo. Trying to figure out how to use the software itself was as confusing as trying to learn Excel.

Some writers love Scrivener and a host of other writing apps (I'm just picking on Scrivener here). If the sidebars and push pins and cork board help you get your writing organized, I'm all for it. But I just felt I would rather spend my time writing instead of learning to navigate yet another piece of software. Eventually you end up with a Word document.

I use Word documents in a similar manner to these writing apps. In writing this book, for example, I created an outline from my mind map (remember, I am a visual writer, I need to see all the trees in the forest). Then I would grab a topic each day and start a new Word document for that topic. I didn't write from beginning to end. Sometimes I felt compelled to word dump on a topic, and that was the topic du jour.

I used descriptive file names so I knew what was in each one. Some files were a few pages long. Others reflected a particularly caffeinated run of 5,000 or more words. After I had about twenty Word documents, created on various days on various topics, I started to assemble them into one Word document like putting a puzzle together.

I understand these writing programs set you up in a template. If your writing follows a template, fine. But does it? Why can't you leave yourself marginal notes using the Comment feature in Track Changes? Why can't you create a footnote in Word to park your research sourcing (and we remove those footnotes in revision and edit)? Why not just delete a bunch of material or park it in a Comment box or delete with tracking on (so the material is visible in the margin and ready for when you want to revive it somewhere else)?

Eventually you will have created your body of work in one Word document. And then the serious revision begins.

You may have a different writing style and preference and don't want to be locked into a template. You might be that audio writer and dictate, and then you have a massive blob of words in a Word document to start your revision process.

You might print out all your chapter material and lay it out on a table (or the floor) and visually put all the pieces together (tip: use headers with the chapter or section name and a page number so you can easily find the material in its proper file).

I have actually done that with one author's manuscript so I could see each chapter. When I was finished putting Humpty Dumpty back together again in a completely different (but logical) order, I had some chapters left over. They didn't make the cut.

If you tend to procrastinate, go ahead and explore those writing programs. And then you'll really have an excuse not to write because you'll be down the rabbit hole of learning a software program.

And about Profanity

Pretty darned difficult to write a book with cops and not use swearing. Or a prison memoir without some salty language. The narrative wouldn't be authentic, and dialogue would sound silly.

Homicide detective Brian Bogdanoff in *Three Bodies Burning* apologized to his mother (but not to his readers) in his acknowledgments, "Sorry, Mom, about all the swear words in the book."

You can warn readers who might be offended by putting a note in the book description: "Contains profanity and adult scenes." Actually, I think that line helps sell books too. People are curious. Amazon will also ask you about adult content when you create your KDP account.

My father was a Marine drill instructor. I grew up with swearing and knew when and when not to punctuate with profanity (most of the time). I'm not offended, but I'm not you. Or your readers. Have you noticed all the books with F*CK in the titles? It was cute for a while. Not so much now.

People swear. Don't be gratuitous about the swearing. Just be true to the freakin' story.

Have I helped you figure out how to get words on paper in a financially rewarding way? Or provided some tips to make the writing process less painful and more fun? I hope so. Once you have your book written and have looked into the editing process, you do need to understand the new world of publishing and why bookstores are a terrible place to buy books (or sell them). And that's the next chapter.

Chapter 13

What I Know about the New World of Publishing

Listen to me when I talk about editing because that's what I do and what I know. Don't always follow what I say about publishing and marketing because those are moving targets. I only know my own experience publishing and marketing my own books—and some experimentation in those realms for some of my authors.

First-time authors sometimes say, "I'm not sure if I want to pursue a traditional publishing contract or just self-publish. I think I'll try a query letter and find an agent." As if self-publishing is a poor second choice when all else fails.

What century are you living in, I ask? Who is giving you bad advice about publishing? Are you open to learning about the new world of publishing?

Warning: the following contains harsh criticism and strong opinions of the author of this book. Traditional publishing is quite simply broken. It used to be you'd try to find a book agent to represent your book and shop your manuscript to the big New York publishing houses with familiar names such as Simon and Schuster and Penguin or Random House. You hoped your typewritten and stapled manuscript would be miraculously plucked from the slush pile, and you'd have instant fame and fortune.

It never worked like that even for the most talented and prestigious authors.

A couple of inventions, with almost as much clout as Gutenberg's printing press, changed the world of publishing forever, as I discussed in the opening of this book. One was digital printing. When I was in high school, the print shop was located across the hall from the journalism room, in room 121. There Mr. Van and the print shop boys (yes, boys, it was vocational training, no girls allowed, it was the dark ages) actually used linotype machines to set hot type (real lead) for pages to print the *Central High Record*.

In room 119, the journalism classroom, I was editor of *The Record*, and we'd type the stories on the old Remington Rands and dilapidated Underwoods with faded ink ribbons and walk the typed stories across the hall to Mr. Van's room where the boys retyped the stories to set hot lead.

Then the presses would run, just like you see on vintage TV shows (and as still happens with big daily newspapers) when monster rolls of paper are imprinted with real ink and then cut and folded.

Fast-forward out of the dark ages of printing to computers. And although the big dailies still prepare the imprinting for printing ink on big rolls of paper, there is no hot type or lead or retyping. The computer files create the pages.

So, too, computers create actual book pages in formats such as PDFs, all electronically, and those electronic files become books printed one at a time in a digital printing process like your computer printer prints out files you send to it. Digital printing. No type, no rolls of paper, efficient, fast. One book at a time.

In those dark ages of book printing, authors who ventured into the uncharted territory of independent publishing and found printers who could put ink on paper and bind them into books had to order hundreds or even thousands of books to make the process cost effective. Even then, each book was expensive to print.

I've known authors who had to move their cars out of the garage so the delivery truck could dump a pallet of books inside the garage for storage. Those books would be there months and years later as the author chipped away at the mountain of books to sell, one by one.

Today, authors can keep their cars in the garage. Digital printing heralded the new age of book publishing. Digital printing changed everything. With just-in-time inventory, books can be printed one by one, packaged, shipped, and delivered to the door of the person ordering a book. Within days. That's the power of Amazon.

The second you buy a book on Amazon, the process begins. Massive digital printing equipment operates much like a giant copier, taking digital book files, covers and interiors, prints them, glues them, and trims the edges, and voila, a book is born. Digital printing. Onto the Amazon delivery trucks, to your door. Two days.

Although I said a couple of inventions changed publishing, the next innovation is not really an invention but a mindset. The stigma of "self-publishing" has gone away. Used to be that anybody who wrote and printed their own book was considered vain (and thus the term *vanity press* was born). It has taken authors years and decades to shed the stigma of the vanity part. I still have authors who consider independent author-publisher publishing a second-rate option, only to be used when all else fails.

I counsel them that traditional publishing is now the second-best option for publishing. And traditional publishing is broken because the model has little to offer an author these days.

"Oh, but the New York publishers will give me a big advance." No, not really. Unless you are Brené Brown or Lee Child or John Bolton, with a blockbuster story or series, the NY publishers are not going to be interested in you. And their gatekeepers, the pond scum of the publishing world, the book agents (don't email me, I am libeling you, so sue me) are like catfish sucking bottom feeders trolling for the next big book. That's not your book.

Bottom line in traditional publishing is this: the only people who make big bucks on your book are the agents and publishers who view your book as a product they can make money on. Your intellectual property—the words that spilled out of your head onto the written page—that's the product you are practically giving them in a traditional publishing deal and letting them make all the moola. Do the math and move on. The bottom line on your book should be going to you, not a greedy agent or publisher who considers your book a commodity, and certainly they aren't arbiters of literary excellence.

"But if a publisher accepts my book, that means it has value." If you are still living in that la-la land where authors think a publisher accepts a book based on the merits of the writing and the literary quality, there's a bridge in Brooklyn you can buy cheap. The publisher accepts a book for publication based on whether the publisher can make money on it. Period. Full stop. No literary masterpieces need apply.

For far too long, the publishing powers that be have created the illusion that they know "good books" when they see them (plucked from a slush pile by a novice college intern, so the old story goes). Doesn't happen.

Agents are now trolling the ranks of independently published books and seeking authors who are making big bucks with big sales on their own and offering them traditional publishing deals (*Fifty Shades* is one example). A reversal of fortune, don't you think? Don't fall for it. You don't need them or the lame horse they rode in on.

I have recently heard about a scam an agent has been peddling. He signs up unsuspecting and hopeful authors for representation. He asks them to revise their proposal a few times. Sends it back for a slight revision to chapter 1 or a refocus of the table of contents. And when the proposal is still not quite right, eventually the agent asks if the author would like to work with a ghostwriter to sharpen that proposal? Yes, of course, the gullible author says, and $3,000 is the ticket to play with no promise that any publisher will ever bite. Please beware. Never ever pay an agent for any services.

Two of my dear authors wrote a timely book at the dawn of an exercise movement. They wrote it, hired me to edit, worked with a designer to design it, printed 5,000 copies, loaded up a van, and traveled the country delivering workshops and hand-selling their book for full retail at $24.95. Do the math. They did well. Then a couple of agents started sniffing around, promised them a big NY publishing contract, even had a little bidding war with publishers who wanted that property.

The authors had the Sally Field syndrome: "They love me. They really love me." They signed on the line, the publisher put on a new back cover but kept everything else the same (not a big capital production outlay for the publisher), paid the authors an advance of several tens of thousands of dollars, published the book under the big NY publisher name, and nothing. Pathetic sales. Miserable sales. Nobody appeared on *Good Morning, America*, as promised.

By the time the next quarter rolled around, the authors had lost their publishing rights (meaning they could not reprint the book themselves and sell it). They had spent much of their advance hoping thousands more in revenue would be coming. It never did. The book died a slow and painful death.

The advance is called an advance against royalties. Until the book sold more than they were paid initially (and let's say their net per book was a buck or so), the authors would never see another dime. Dime? Heck, they never saw another penny. Most books never "earn out" in that broken business.

Why would you want a publishing contract like that? What can a big NY publisher do for you? Not much more than you can do for yourself. As an independently published author, you can get your book everywhere the publishing companies can: bookstores, Amazon, boutiques, libraries (okay, maybe not Costco or Sam's Club, but the dirty little secret is that most of the books you see at Costco or Walmart are never sold and return through distributors and wholesalers to the publishers and end up in landfills). I rest my case.

The Worst Place to Buy a Book

Authors tell me they want to see their books on a bookstore shelf. They want to walk up to the appropriate section and see their treasure and life's work displayed for all the world to see.

Yes, I've had that experience, and it's gratifying—until you realize that you really want your book in the hands of someone who is standing at the checkout counter with a credit card, not languishing on a shelf in a bookstore surrounded by thousands of other books, vying for the attention of someone, anyone, a forlorn orphan. Only to be returned to the publisher as unsold.

And that's the problem. Bookstores only carry hot titles from a dwindling number of major (and some minor) publishers. Yours won't stand out unless you stand in front of the shelf and collar people as they walk by. Oh, that's called a book signing, and the last thing you want to do is have a stack of your books on a table in a bookstore hoping people will ask you to sign it for them. Lonely. Humiliating. [Fill in your adjective.]

Moving on. Bookstores don't own their inventory. It's a wonderful business model if you're a bookstore. Get merchandise in. Try to sell it. And, oh, if it doesn't sell, then ship it back. Simple. No cash outlay to fill the shelves.

So if you work with distributors and wholesalers who also have their hands in your pockets and get your books into bookstores, figure that up to 90 percent of those books will come back on the same trucks they went in on. But this time they'll be damaged because somebody spilled coffee on your book in the coffee shop. And then you have paid return shipping, and you end up selling used goods in used goods venues such as Amazon new/used or the church rummage sale.

And if, OMG, your book does sell in bookstores, do the math. Your profit just might cover your cost of goods sold and shipped. Maybe. Even John Grisham gets about a dollar for each of his hard cover books sold.

Please, my friends, who still have jobs at Barnes & Noble, don't email me. I know your plight. My husband used to work on the sinking ship at Borders (remember them?). Authors, the world is your oyster, just open it to find new venues to sell your books.

Bookstores, therefore, are a terrible place to sell books, and the newest numbers show that people rarely buy books at bookstores. They buy books on Amazon. Jeff Bezos is not on my Christmas card list, but Amazon is where books are printed (on Amazon's printing platform called KDP) and sold.

Think about where people buy books. Where did you buy your last book? I doubt it was in a bookstore. Most people in my writing classes report the current book they are reading was either purchased on Amazon or checked out at the library.

Does it matter who publishes your book? In my writing class, I do an exercise with the group. I pass out a number of books and ask the students to tell the group about the book: the title, the subject, the publisher, and the cover.

I have carefully selected some books that have been expertly independently published. They have stunning covers, highly descriptive titles, lovely interior layouts. After we've discussed the look and feel of these books, I ask, "Does it matter who published these books?" And the answer is, of course, it doesn't matter who the publisher is. Only the DIY-looking, homemade covers and interior designs with tight gutters and poor type design stand out as the amateur undertakings they are, and these are the books that give self-publishing a black eye.

When was the last time you picked up a book and checked out the name of the publisher? Like never. You look for a subject matter of interest. Check. You determine the subject matter from the title and subtitle and look of the cover. Check. And you turn the book over and read the all-important back cover for further explanation, and that's where the book is either taken up to the counter and purchased or put back on the shelf or table in the bookstore, at the library, or clicked BUY NOW on Amazon. Am I right?

Yes, but. Except on Amazon, you can use the book description page to get even more information. You can read the Amazon ranking, if that's important to you. You can see other similar books. You can read reviews from other readers. You can quickly see the publication year if recency is important to you. You can see other books by the author and read more about the author too.

And the name of the publisher is tucked away on a small line in the middle of the Amazon page, because, well, who the hell cares?

The Rise and Promise of Independent Publishing

Before I leave this topic of publishing, let me bore you with my diatribe on the three essential truths (you never knew) about independent publishing.

TRUTH #1: SELF-PUBLISHING IS EASIER THAN YOU THINK.

No longer do authors have to order large offset print runs, clear out their garages, park the car on the street, and chip away selling a pallet of books. Amazon's KDP digital printing for just-in-time inventory has revolutionized the book business. Which leads to truth #2 ...

TRUTH #2: YOU HAVE COMPLETE CONTROL OF THE PUBLISHING PROCESS.

How many books do you need? With digital uploading to such publishing platforms as Amazon's KDP or Ingram-Spark, as an independent author-publisher, you control the cover design, the interior design, and number of books to order (as few as one or as many as hundreds) at a time. And making editorial changes once that glaring typo jumps off the page and bites you is simple and easy (sort of). Don't you want a say in how your cover looks?

TRUTH #3: YOU OWN YOUR OWN SMALL BUSINESS.

Welcome to the world of self-publishing, micro publishing, independent publishing, hybrid publishing—the new stigma-free mainstream. Writing the book, you will soon realize, was the easy part. Keeping all the profits? Priceless.

Class dismissed.

Don't Be That Author—A Short Course in Author/Editor Etiquette

You've heard about difficult people being called "Karen." Karen is the entitled suburban yoga mom who doesn't get her way in the restaurant or coffee shop or retail store who asks to see the manager. That's Karen.

I admit, I've been that Karen without the yoga pants. Maybe at Target, not sure if that was me.

But do you really want to be *that* author? The one who sends your editor ten emails a day? The one who nitpicks about commas or insists on a particularly ineffective cover design? The author who includes song lyrics (against the sound advice of your editor)? The author who lifts material from others without permissions and appropriate attribution? Who disappears for months at a time and then pushes the editor to meet a self-imposed deadline? Who writes another two chapters after a final edit? Or, worse, who makes edits after a final edit but doesn't get those edits edited?

That author.

I speak from experience with them. I have lived through all those scenarios. Among ourselves, we editors love to trade pain-in-the-ass author stories. "You wouldn't believe what this author did," we vent. We shake our heads. We breathe a sigh of relief knowing our name is not on that book anywhere.

Here is our editorial take on Karen authors: You hired a professional editor to perform a professional service. Why not let us do what we do best and that's to make you look fabulous, to help you create a commercial-quality book that can compete in a crowded marketplace?

That said, I always tell authors this: You will win every disagreement we have. Your opinion counts more than mine. You can do whatever you wish with your book. You decide the fate of your book.

I have only walked away from three manuscripts over editorial disagreements (so far). I would not move forward with editorial decisions that compromised my integrity or that I felt were too detrimental to the author's credibility. One example was an author who admitted she embellished her story in a memoir and would not label it fiction. Another was an author whose book was just a compilation of quotations from other people, and he had not sought permission for use.

For every Karen, there are plenty of not-Karens. One author recently sent me an email about our collaboration on his book that said, "My confidence in you makes it easy." Best compliment ever.

We all want to work with more authors like that.

Should Your Editor Sign a Nondisclosure Agreement (NDA)?

I have been asked to sign an NDA a few times, and I have no problem doing so. As an editor, I am in no danger of telling anyone else about what you are writing (presumably so no one else steals the idea). But nondisclosure and confidentiality is really just commonsense for editors with a signed agreement or without.

Can Your Editor Help You Edit Other Materials Associated with Your Book?

Yes. An editor can be available to edit all the collateral items that go with book writing and publishing and marketing, like these:

- Your back cover, which can become a longer Amazon description
- Your author bio
- Jacket copy if you create a hard cover book with a dust jacket
- Your book or brand website content (sadly, I see too many author/book websites with major typos and misspellings, even though they look sharp enough)
- Marketing materials such as a postcard or business card
- Press release
- Blogs
- Other social media posts

I'm a journalist, so writing some of these items isn't scary to me at all. I do like to have the authors take a stab at a bio or a blog. Their name, after all, is on the material.

Will My Editor Tell Me if
My Writing Sucks?

"I just want to know if my writing is any good," I hear often.

Aha. The fear factor. Author Anne Lamott and others give you permission to write a shitty (her word) first draft. So do it. You don't have to show it to anyone. Just bang it out. Even my idol Stephen King roughs out his work with the door closed. It's the second draft that gets shown to selected critical readers.

You've got to climb to the top of the ladder on the high diving board and just jump. Show smaller sections to trusted readers. Listen to many, not just one. And certainly not someone who is related to you by marriage or DNA. Look at my discussion of beta readers in chapter 10. They can tell you if your writing sucks. Frankly, I've never told an author their writing sucks nor have beta readers gone that far.

Look for patterns of comments (*your dialogue needs to be shorter; your descriptions aren't quite giving me a picture; I had trouble following the plot; why did you spend so much time talking about your mother*). Then take action with a red pencil, Track Changes, or scissors.

Now about that "good" thing. Good to one person is "best book ever" to another or absolutely horrible to another. That's why one book does not fit all. To an editor, like me, one measure of good is mechanical (Are commas in the right place?) and another is substantive (Is the manuscript well organized or scattered? Does the title grab attention? Are characters developed?). Tell your story. Your readers and the marketplace will be the judge of "good."

Chapter 15

The End

When you type "The End" and you think you're finished, the fun just begins. The world needs to find your book and read it.

Go back to your original reasons for writing a book: to impart wisdom, to help others, to leave a legacy, to get the words out, to share experiences, to tell your story.

Now it's time to find the target readers and introduce them to your book. My job as editor ends at this point. I shove you out of the cozy editorial nest with my best wishes and watch you fly away.

Please take your book to the next level by exploring the many experts on book marketing. Many have written helpful books. Some stage informative webinars. Others also offer boot camps and challenges. You'll find yourself immersed in the world of Amazon Ads, BookBub Ads, Google Ads, Facebook Ads, email lists, and a bazillion other ways you can spend money to sell books (with the hope of making it all back and more).

My only caution is to cautiously step into the rough and tumble waters of book marketing one small step at a time. Become an expert on Amazon, carefully write and execute your Amazon description page. Claim your author page at Author Central. Craft smart ads for your book for Amazon Ads. Gone are the days when an author needs to sit in a bookstore or library with a stack of books and hope somebody comes to buy a book so you can sign it.

Set up events where you speak on your topic or your story to a target audience. You are only limited by your imagination. You wrote your story, now sell it.

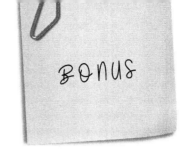

Checklist for Authors to Fine-Tune a Manuscript before Editing Begins

This section is the reason you are reading this book. Here is the information authors want and need and can't find anywhere else.

I have discussed many of these Checklist items earlier in this book. Use this Checklist to prepare your final draft *before* you work with an editor. The cleaner your manuscript is going into an edit with a professional editor, the cleaner your work will be after an edit. Correcting and fixing typos and problems when your book is in production can be expensive, time-consuming, frustrating, and just plain foolish.

A well-prepared manuscript allows an editor to spend their time (and your money) on fine-tuning at a higher level for content and sentence-level fixes rather than spending time deleting double spacing and addressing formatting issues.

 WORDS

☐ **Problem words:** Search and replace when you used and overused my pet peeve words. Search now (control F) for these nonwords: *good*, *great*, *very*, *really*, *pretty*, and *things*. Replace them with stronger words or simply delete *really*, *very*, and *pretty*.

☐ **Sensitivity read:** Have you reviewed your writing for sensitivity to racial, ethnic, gender, sexuality, cultural, age, appearance, ability, and health terms to be inclusive or hired a sensitivity editor to review?

☐ **Misspelled, misunderstood, or misused words from A to Z:** If you really want to do a pre-edit polish on specific words, do a find (control F) to look for these words (and there are plenty more) that are often misspelled, misunderstood, or misused (or leave this task for your editor). Among all the words authors stumble over, I find these most commonly need attention:

- Acknowledgments (The section where you thank everybody who helped you. It is not spelled Acknowledgements.)
- affect, effect (If you struggle with these, your editor will correct you.)
- aisles, isles (As in grocery aisles and isles or islands)
- backward (not backwards), same with toward (not towards)
- complementary, complimentary (If the gray sweater goes nicely with black pants, the sweater is

complementary. If you give someone a compliment about their outfit, you're being complimentary. And if breakfast at the hotel is free with your stay, the meal is complimentary unless the waffles are cold and hard, then breakfast is a disaster.)

- fewer, less (Irks me when I see this sign in the grocery checkout aisle: *Less than 12 items*. I always remind the manager about the mistake. It's *fewer than 12 items* because you can count them, and the shopper with 13 items will always be in front of you. But who's counting?)

- Foreword (This is the correct spelling of the section at the front of the book that nobody needs, not Forward or something else.)

- gray, grey (We are writing in American English, use the American spelling: gray.)

- its and it's (The biggest of the big misuses, and I think it's because the grammar checker flags these or self-corrects. The second is a contraction of it is. If *it is* makes sense in your sentence, then you can use it's.)

- lets and let's (The second is a contraction of let us, so if *let us* makes sense in your sentence, then you have used let's correctly.)

- stationary, stationery (I always remember something not moving or standing stationary because stand has the *a*, while stationery is the pretty monogrammed paper your grandmother used to use to send you notes with a couple of bucks enclosed.)

- that, which (A finer point but often misused. It's about nonrestrictive and restrictive clauses that will make your eyes glaze over. Best left to your editor. But *which* clauses are set off with a comma.)

- their, there, they're (The first is possessive. The second is a direction (over there). The third is a contraction of they are, and if *they are* makes sense, you are correctly using they're.)
- toward (not towards)
- who, whom (I find these difficult to work with and even when a sentence is correct but sounds wrong, I advise you to rewrite the sentence. I do. And who am I to argue with that?)
- whose, who's (The second is a contraction of *who is*. If you can substitute *who is* and the sentence makes sense, you are correctly using who's.)
- you're, your (The first is a contraction of *you are*. The second is possessive.)

☐ **Fact checking**: Did you look up spellings and facts, names and dates?

☐ **Spelling and grammar checkers**: Did you resist the temptation to run a spell check or make changes based on flagged items (knowing these are often incorrectly flagged with Word's spelling and grammar checkers)?

☐ **Internal notes**: Have you removed any internal notes to yourself in the manuscript?

 FORMAT

☐ **File format:** Is your final manuscript in a Word document file (extension of .doc or .docx) and not from a Mac (.pages)? Or a Google Doc? Ask your editor which file format they prefer to edit.

☐ **Spacing:** Have you removed all the double spaces after punctuation between sentences? Just one space between sentences is needed. Use the find and replace feature carefully.

☐ **Returns:** Make sure you have no stray returns (called carriage returns or Enters).

☐ **Other formatting:** Most editors can reformat easily to their preference for font size and type. I prefer Times New Roman 12 point with normal margins and spacing between lines of 1.5 or 2.0. But this is not critical. Just easier to read.

☐ **Tracking:** If you were using Track Changes or marginal Comments in Word, have you accepted all tracking and removed all Comments? Exceptions would be specific instructions to your editor left as marginal Comments. Learn to use Track Changes (under the Review tab in Word).

☐ **New pages:** Does each new chapter and part and section start on a new page? Insert a hard Page Break at these points (Ctrl+Enter). Don't simply use a series of Enters to break a page.

- [ ] **Italics:** Have you put the appropriate words in italics, such as titles of books? Have you overused italics and need to remove some of it? Or put quotation marks around words for emphasis and overdone it? Rarely use what are called scare quotes to emphasize a word. Save that for when you might use "air quotes" if you were speaking.

- [ ] **Boldface:** Use sparingly and put any words or phrases you wish to have in bold in **boldface**.

- [ ] **Underline:** Remove any underlining. Books do not use underlining.

- [ ] **Paragraphing:** Do you have huge long paragraphs? Like a full page for just one paragraph? These will be gray walls in your manuscript and highly unappealing to a reader. Break up long runs into new paragraphs.

- [ ] **Subheadings:** If you have subheadings, are they consistent, do they have initial caps, and if you have more than one level of subheading, is it clear from the font and size that there is a hierarchy?

 PARTS OF THE BOOK

- [ ] **Parts of the book:** Have you written and included all the parts your book requires?

  - Praise pages/endorsements
  - Title page
  - Copyright page
  - Dedication (optional)

- Contents (label it Contents, not Table of Contents)
- Chapters (numbered with chapter titles for nonfiction)
- End matter such as References, Resources, Notes
- Acknowledgments
- About the Author
- Back cover copy

☐ **Titles:** Do all the chapter titles exactly match the titles on the Contents page? Do not put page numbers there.

 ## PUNCTUATION

☐ **Quotation marks:** Have you overused quotation marks around words? Remove them. If you want to signify emphasis, italics can be used sparingly.

☐ **Exclamation marks:** Use too many exclamation marks and they lose their punch. Let the words be the punch. No more than five exclamation marks in an entire book. Seriously!

☐ **Punctuation within quotation marks:** Is most punctuation within ending quotation marks? The editor can sort out any of those rare instances where punctuation goes outside.

☐ **Bulleted and numbered lists:** Are your bulleted lists consistent with all phrases or all sentences with ending punctuation? Do you really need a numbered list (use only if the steps are in a sequence)?

GRAPHICS AND ILLUSTRATIONS

☐ **Photos, graphics, illustrations:** If you inserted any photos or other graphics such as charts and graphs or cartoons, the editor will assume they go where you have placed them. Big graphic files can be kept in a separate file, not in the manuscript itself. Otherwise, have you indicated where, in the text, such elements would go with bracketed notes like this and a caption: [INSERT photo 45 here: My sister (at left) and I pose with the mules during a trip to the Grand Canyon in 2012.]? Have you written and included a caption for every graphic element? Did you identify who is in the photo (left to right), when the photo was taken, where?

AND FINALLY...

☐ **Celebrate:** When you finally, literally, put down the figurative pen or turn off the computer, celebrate. Sigh of relief. Smile. Insert happy face emoji here.

☐ **Contact your editor:** I'll be waiting.

Resources I Recommend for Further Advice on Writing and Editing

What? You were expecting a simple list here? A detailed bibliography? What fun is that?

So there you are. Searching on Amazon or in the library for books on writing. Surely there's a book that can tell you how and what to write. It will literally pull the words out of your brain.

No. Wasting time hanging around bookstores looking for the pot of gold won't get *your* book written. Only you can do the work. It's like hanging around a gym and watching others clang the weights and sweat on the treadmills and thinking you'll get six-pack abs and lose weight.

Ain't happenin'.

But ... but ... but my adult writing students often ask, surely there's a book that can help me get organized and start writing.

Other than doing free writing, mind mapping, writing all the time, making lists, chaining your laptop to your waist, and drinking Red Bull, I do recommend three writers and their books, if you insist:

- Anne Lamott's *Bird by Bird: Some Instructions on Writing and Life* is easy and quick to read. She gives you permission to bang it out and write (in her words) that shitty first draft. She also gives guidance on how to handle sensitive topics such as abuse and abusers.
- In *Writing Down the Bones,* Natalie Goldberg assembles the sugar, flour, eggs, and vanilla. But do you have a cake yet? No. She gives some useful pointers to get your cake baking.
- And, of course, Stephen King. His autobiography and writing guide, *On Writing*, is a classic. Make sure you buy a paper copy, not ebook version, because you'll want to dog-ear, highlight, and sticky note this thing to death (hmm, a common theme of his). He's a master. You'll learn a lot about him and about writing and discipline—and maybe something about yourself as a writer.

If you want to take a peek at the *Chicago Manual of Style*, it's online at www.ChicagoManualOfStyle.org. You need a paid subscription to search online, however.

I use the Merriam-Webster unabridged dictionary online, but a current college dictionary should serve you well.

If you need guidance on fact checking, try these resources: *The Chicago Guide to Fact-Checking* by Brooke Borel and *The Fact Checker's Bible* by Sarah Harrison Smith.

And my go-to legal eagle Helen Sedwick's *Self-Publisher's Legal Handbook* for all things copyright and permissions, fair use, song lyrics, poetry, and libel and slander.

Reedsy.com has a deep resource for blogs and webinars on writing, editing, and design. I enjoy their Facebook live book cover critiques.

Publishing guru Jane Friedman blogs and stages webinars at www.JaneFriedman.com.

I edited Jennifer Lovett's *Social Media for Authors: Book Marketing for Authors Who'd Rather Write* and learned a lot about the power of social media in book sales.

You'll find other book publishing industry experts to follow. Zoom in on free webinars on writing, on selling books, and on how to use Amazon Ads, Google Ads, and Facebook Ads. Once the writing is finished and your book is up on Amazon through KDP, the fun begins with marketing in earnest.

So why are you still reading this? Get busy writing.

Acknowledgments

Books don't write themselves. Everything I am and everything I know came from somewhere or someone. I just happened to put it all together at this point in time, during a global pandemic, when everyone was home writing books.

I like to tell people I'm a boring person, with not a particularly interesting backstory, but I have met so many insanely fascinating people, I know their stories because I helped them write and publish them. It's as if I lived my life through them vicariously.

I have, therefore, traveled the world, met presidents and kings and saints, survived the Holocaust, was diagnosed as bipolar, was a party girl with Frank Sinatra, recovered from incest, helped lepers in Mother Teresa's leper colony in Yemen, did eight balls backstage with rock stars, nearly crashed a plane in China, guarded a US president, schmoozed with a funeral home director, went on patrol in Vietnam, edited a Hollywood screenwriter, fell in love in Italy, formed successful start-ups, sold a ton of real estate, helped people with anxiety or marriages on the rocks, had my own Twitch stream, ran a major corporation as CEO, built a Las Vegas casino, arrested bad guys, shot and killed a drug dealer, and did time in prison for bank robbery. I thank these authors for being my editing clients, for letting me dig through their lives, and for letting me push them to write their best books ever.

I mention many of these people whom I call "my authors" in this book. They graciously allowed me to share their stories and examples.

To all the eager learners who attended my classes in how to write a book, thank you for letting me think I really know what I'm talking about. I appreciate your kind attention—or was it the Krispy Kremes I brought to class?

To my beta readers: Judy Lund-Bell, Vicky DeCoster, Jenny Kate, Barbara Lynn Vannoy, Elizabeth Sheridan, Chris Meyer, Mary Anne Shepard, Shelby Janke, Dennis Geelan, Catherine Rymsha, Patricia Heinicke, Susan Spero, and Scott Rossignol—and I thought I had nailed it. You guys were tough on me.

To my business colleague, co-instructor, guru, Lisa Pelto of Concierge Publishing Services. The universe brought us together to collaborate on so many books. I learned much from you about this crazy world of books. We have plenty more chapters to write.

To my mentor Lisa Drucker, the ultimate wordsmith who can finish the NYT crossword puzzle in record time.

I am grateful to my coauthor and friend Dr. Edward Creagan who generously offered me coauthorship on "our" books. We have another book in the works. Follow him at www.AskDoctorEd.com and on Twitter @EdwardCreagan. He gives wise advice on medical issues and on life, and he allows me to edit his perceptive blog posts.

Thank you, Tom Liggett, for the lovely poem I used in the dedication. Your memoir (*Mozart in the Garden*) still haunts me.

To Miss Julia Barker, my beloved high school English teacher, who made punctuation practically fun. To Mr. Van who named me Editor-in-Chief of the school newspaper and confirmed my career choice as a journalist. To my grandfather from whom I received my love of words. To my grandmother who inspired me to write a cookbook in her honor (www.Chewish.com) and celebrate our family over a bowl of matzo ball soup.

To Scott because of all the years, two kids, two grandkids, six dogs, and for giving me space and not murdering each other during lockdown.

That's my village.

About the Author

Sandra Wendel is a highly experienced book editor who specializes in helping authors write, polish, and publish their nonfiction manuscripts.

Her greatest joy in editing is working with authors who have a story to tell. She has worked with Holocaust survivors (an honor and a privilege), a Secret Service agent, a bank robber, entrepreneurs, an eighties rock groupie, a homicide detective, a narcotics sergeant, a beat cop, funeral home director, real estate agents, doctors, lawyers, abused, military veterans, parents, therapists, a Pulitzer Prize–nominated journalist, visionary, CEOs, coaches, Vegas party girl, historians, and even more fascinating ordinary people with extraordinary stories.

One of her authors asked her how many books she has edited. Hundreds, for sure, and perhaps well over a thousand. Her specialties include memoir, true crime, health and self-help, and business/leadership.

She is a published author herself, sharing the authorship of two award-winning, empowering consumer health books with Edward T. Creagan, MD, a physician from Mayo Clinic (www.AskDoctorEd.com): *How Not to Be My Patient: A Physician's Secrets for Staying Healthy and Surviving Any Diagnosis* and *Farewell: Vital End-of-Life Questions with Candid Answers from a Leading Palliative and Hospice Physician.* She also wrote a cookbook tribute to her grandmother: *Chewish* (www.Chewish.com).

Sandra teaches highly popular continuing education classes at Metropolitan Community College in Omaha, Nebraska, called How to Write Your Book and How to Write Your Story (memoir). She is a member of the Editorial Freelancers Association, ACES: The Society for Editing, Nonfiction Authors Association, and reviews books under consideration for NFAA and Eric Hoffer Awards.

She kayaks on her little lake in Nebraska until it ices over in winter and often reads a book a day (something trashy or a legal thriller) for escape and tries not to notice poor punctuation and editing.

Visit her website at www.SandraWendel.com. Email her at Sandra@SandraWendel.com. Join the Facebook group at FirstTimeAuthorsClub.

Thank you for reading my book.

It means the world to me that you have taken time to read my words of advice for first-time authors. I know you have hundreds of choices when you buy books and spend your valuable time and money. Thank you, dear readers, for giving me both your time and money. I hope I have overdelivered.

I speak with first-time authors on the phone and via email every day. You inspire me with your eagerness to become authors, and I hope you have found wisdom (or at least answers) in this book.

Like every author, I **welcome your feedback** on this book (even the typos, and a few are planted in the manuscript as a test). Please email me Sandra@SandraWendel. com. Connect with me on Twitter @SandraWendel. And of course at my website: www.SandraWendel.com.

Follow my occasional **posts** on writing on LinkedIn, and **join** the Facebook page for first-time authors (we all were first-time authors at one time) FirstTimeAuthorsClub.

If you still have questions or would like to **work with me** on your book or have me **evaluate your manuscript** for editing, I would love to hear from you.

If you would like to share your thoughts about this book with other first-time authors, kindly leave a **review on Amazon**. Reviews are gold for every author, and I wish you a gazillion five-star reviews for your book when it comes out.

≣ Write on!

Made in the USA
Middletown, DE
07 December 2021